10,000 USEFUL ADJECTIVES IN ENGLISH

TYPES, DEGREES AND FORMATION OF ADJECTIVES

MANIK JOSHI

<u>Dedication</u>

THIS BOOK IS

DEDICATED

TO THOSE

WHO REALIZE

THE POWER OF ENGLISH

AND WANT TO

LEARN IT

SINCERELY

<u>Copyright</u> <u>Notice</u>

****

<u>IMPORTANT</u> <u>NOTE</u>

This Book is Part of a Series
SERIES Name: "English Daily Use"
[A Forty-Book Series]
BOOK Number: 37
BOOK Title: "10,000 Useful Adjectives In English"

****

Table of Contents

01. <u>What Are Adjectives</u>

DEFINITION: Adjectives are words that modify or describe nouns: wonderful, great, red, powerless. They can also describe the quantity of nouns: half, many, few, millions, eleven. An adjective can be put before the noun. This is called attributive position. An adjective can also be put after the verb to be (is/are/am/was/were) or verb of sense (look/feel/taste/smell etc.). This is called predicative position.

Example Sentences:
He left behind a **wonderful** *legacy*. (*adjective: wonderful | noun: legacy*)
It was a **needless** *exercise* in the first place. (*adjective: needless | noun: exercise*)
Clinical *trials* for vaccine showed positive results. (*adjective: clinical | noun: trials*)
Not **many** *players* receive contracts of **10** years or more. (*adjective: many | noun: players*)

In the sentences above, the adjectives come immediately before the nouns they modify. Here, they are called **attributive adjectives.**

But adjectives can do more than just modify nouns. They can act as a complement to linking verbs or the verb 'to be'. In this case, they are called **predicative adjectives.** (Complement is a word, phrase or clause that is required to complete the meaning of some other element in the clause.)

Example Sentences:
All these students *are* **studious.**
This house *is* **bigger** than that one.
Reading *is* **easier** than writing.
Citrus *tastes* **sour.**
He *feels* **good.**
She *looked* **tired.**
It *seems* **impossible.**

In the sentences above, the adjectives were used **predicatively.**

THE <u>ADJECTIVE</u> <u>SLOTS</u>

01. Attributive Adjectives
02. Predicate Adjectives

Adjectives are used either attributively or predicatively. In other words, there are two types of adjective slots. These two slots are found in three locations:

(A). Attributive Adjective in the Subject (Modifier to Noun)
Example Sentence: An **intelligent** *person* is admired. *('Intelligent' is an adjective)*
(Subject -- An **intelligent** *person* | Predicate -- is admired.)

(B). Attributive Adjective in the Predicate: (Modifier to Noun)
Example Sentence: He is an **intelligent** *person*. *('Intelligent' is an adjective)*
(Subject -- He | Predicate -- is an **intelligent** *person*.)

(C). Predicate Adjective in the Predicate: (Predicate Complement -- Adjective)
Example Sentence: He is **intelligent**. *('Intelligent' is an adjective)*
(Subject -- He | Predicate -- is **intelligent**.)

ALSO NOTE:
PREDICATE COMPLEMENT— NOUN
A *person* of high **intelligence** is admired *('intelligence' is a noun)*

IT + BE + ADJECTIVE
Adjectives can act as a complement to linking verbs or the verb *"to be"*. Additional Examples of 'Predicate Complement -- Adjective' are as follows:

Example Sentences:

Make small goals that *are* **obtainable.**
This target *is* **achievable**
This battle *is* **needless.**
Not all fingers *are* **equal.**

COORDINATE ADJECTIVES

Adjectives are said to be coordinate if they modify the same noun in a sentence. Coordinate adjectives should be separated by a comma or the word 'and'.

Example Sentences:
Warm *and* sunny conditions continued as the new week began.
I am passionate about keeping my home a **clean *and* safe** place for me.
All my friends are **calm *and* composed.**
His communication skills *are* **effective *and* efficient.**
It is a **treacherous *and* risky** *place* to explore.
We need **systematic *and* sustained** action to secure the removal of discriminatory laws and regulations.
His **sudden *and* unexpected** *death* shocked the country.
Without **substantial *and* verifiable** *proof,* a court is likely to rule against your position.
Weather hampered **search *and* recovery** *efforts* for three people who went missing in separate incidents
Over the last **10** years, he has proved himself to be a **reliable *and* trustworthy** *partner* to us.

Note: Sometimes, an adjective and a noun form a single semantic unit, which is then modified by another adjective. In this case, the adjectives are not coordinate and should not be separated by a comma or 'and'.

Example Sentence:
She is fond of her **new yellow** car.
In the above sentence, "her **new and yellow** car" doesn't sound right because we aren't talking about a car that is both new and yellow. We are taking about a yellow car that is new.

02. 10,000 Useful Adjectives

NOTE: All of the following words are definitely used as adjectives, but many of them can also be used as nouns, verbs, etc.

02a. Useful Adjectives -- 'A'

1. abandoned / **2**. abashed / **3**. aberrant / **4**. abhorrent / **5**. abiding / **6**. ablaze / **7**. able / **8**. able-bodied / **9**. abnormal / **10**. abominable / **11**. abortive / **12**. above / **13**. above board / **14**. above-mentioned / **15**. abrasive / **16**. abrupt / **17**. absent / **18**. absent-minded / **19**. absolute / **20**. absorbable / **21**. absorbed / **22**. absorbent / **23**. absorbing / **24**. abstemious / **25**. abstracted / **26**. abundant / **27**. abusive / **28**. abysmal / **29**. academic / **30**. academically bright / **31**. accented / **32**. acceptable / **33**. accessible / **34**. accessory / **35**. accidental / **36**. accident-prone / **37**. accommodating / **38**. accomplished / **39**. accountable / **40**. accredited / **41**. accumulative / **42**. accurate / **43**. accursed / **44**. accusatory / **45**. accusing / **46**. accustomed / **47**. achievable / **48**. achy / **49**. acidic / **50**. acne-prone / **51**. acoustic / **52**. acoustical / **53**. acquainted / **54**. acquisitive / **55**. acrimonious / **56**. acrobatic / **57**. acrylic / **58**. acting / **59**. actionable / **60**. action-oriented / **61**. action-packed / **62**. active / **63**. actively zealous / **64**. actual / **65**. acute / **66**. acutely conscious / **67**. acyclic / **68**. adamant / **69**. adamantine / **70**. adaptable / **71**. adaptive / **72**. addicted / **73**. addiction-related / **74**. addictive / **75**. additional / **76**. addressable / **77**. adept / **78**. adhesive / **79**. adjacent / **80**. adjustable / **81**. administrative / **82**. admirable / **83**. admissible / **84**. adopted / **85**. adoptive / **86**. adorable / **87**. adoring / **88**. adrift / **89**. adroit / **90**. adult / **91**. adulterous / **92**. adult-oriented / **93**. advanced / **94**. advancing / **95**. advantaged / **96**. advantageous / **97**. adventitious / **98**. adventure-loving / **99**. adventuresome / **100**. adventurous / **101**. adverbial / **102**. adversarial / **103**. adverse / **104**. adversely hit / **105**. advisable / **106**. advisory / **107**. aerial / **108**. aerobic / **109**. aeronautical / **110**. aesthetic / **111**. aesthetical / **112**. aesthetically designed / **113**. affable / **114**. affected / **115**. affective / **116**. affiliated / **117**. affirmative / **118**. affluent / **119**. affordable / **120**.

afloat / **121**. afoot / **122**. aforementioned / **123**. aforethought / **124**. afraid / **125**. African / **126**. after / **127**. aged / **128**. ageing / **129**. ageless / **130**. age-old / **131**. age-related / **132**. agglomerate / **133**. agglutinative / **134**. aggravated / **135**. aggregate / **136**. aggressive / **137**. aggrieved / **138**. aghast / **139**. agitated / **140**. aglow / **141**. agog / **142**. agonized / **143**. agonizing / **144**. agrarian / **145**. agreeable / **146**. agriculture-related / **147**. ailing / **148**. aimless / **149**. airborne / **150**. air-conditioned / **151**. air-cooled / **152**. air-filled / **153**. airless / **154**. airsick / **155**. airtight / **156**. air-to-air / **157**. air-to-ground / **158**. air-to-surface / **159**. airworthy / **160**. airy / **161**. airy-fairy / **162**. ajar / **163**. alarmed / **164**. alarming / **165**. alarmist / **166**. alcohol-fuelled / **167**. alcoholic / **168**. alert / **169**. alfresco / **170**. algae-infested / **171**. algae-ridden / **172**. algebraic / **173**. alien / **174**. alight / **175**. alike / **176**. alive / **177**. alkaline / **178**. all-action / **179**. all-around / **180**. all-consuming / **181**. allergic / **182**. allied / **183**. alligator-infested / **184**. all-important / **185**. all-in / **186**. all-inclusive / **187**. all-night / **188**. all-or-nothing / **189**. all-out / **190**. all-over / **191**. allowable / **192**. all-party / **193**. all-powerful / **194**. all-purpose / **195**. all-star / **196**. all-ticket / **197**. alluring / **198**. allusive / **199**. alluvial / **200**. all-weather / **201**. almighty / **202**. alone / **203**. aloof / **204**. alphabetic / **205**. alphabetical / **206**. alphanumeric / **207**. alphanumerical / **208**. alright / **209**. alternate / **210**. alternative / **211**. amateurish / **212**. amatory / **213**. amazed / **214**. amazing / **215**. ambassadorial / **216**. ambidextrous / **217**. ambient / **218**. ambiguous / **219**. ambitious / **220**. ambivalent / **221**. ambulatory / **222**. amenable / **223**. amendable / **224**. amenities-deprived / **225**. amenities-filled / **226**. American / **227**. American-made / **228**. amiable / **229**. amicable / **230**. amiss / **231**. amoral / **232**. amorous / **233**. amorphous / **234**. amphibious / **235**. ample / **236**. amused / **237**. amusing / **238**. analogous / **239**. analogue / **240**. analphabetic / **241**. analytic / **242**. analytical / **243**. analyzable / **244**. anaphoric / **245**. anarchic / **246**. anarchical / **247**. anatomical / **248**. ancient / **249**. ancillary / **250**. androgynous / **251**. anecdotal / **252**. anemic / **253**. anesthetic / **254**. angelic / **255**. angelical / **256**. Anglophobic / **257**. angry / **258**. angst-ridden / **259**. angular / **260**. anhydrous / **261**. animal-centric / **262**. animal-loving / **263**. animate / **264**. annoyance-causing / **265**. annoyed / **266**. annoying / **267**. annual / **268**. annular / **269**. anodyne / **270**. anomalous / **271**. anonymous / **272**.

anorexic / **273**. answerable / **274**. antagonistic / **275**. antecedent / **276**. antediluvian / **277**. anterior / **278**. anthrax-infested / **279**. anthropocentric / **280**. anthropomorphic / **281**. anti-anxiety / **282**. antibacterial / **283**. anti-bacterial / **284**. anti-begging / **285**. antibiotic-resistant / **286**. anti-cheating / **287**. anti-choice / **288**. anti-cholera / **289**. anticipatory / **290**. anticlockwise / **291**. anti-competitive / **292**. anti-copying / **293**. anti-corruption / **294**. anti-doping / **295**. anti-drug / **296**. anti-encroachment / **297**. anti-extremism / **298**. anti-graft / **299**. anti-hate / **300**. anti-inflammatory / **301**. anti-liquor / **302**. anti-littering / **303**. anti-malarial / **304**. anti-national / **305**. anti-party / **306**. antipathetic / **307**. anti-people / **308**. anti-personnel / **309**. anti-poaching / **310**. anti-pollution / **311**. antiquarian / **312**. antiquated / **313**. antique / **314**. antiretroviral / **315**. anti-riot / **316**. anti-rowdy / **317**. anti-sabotage / **318**. anti-satellite / **319**. anti-Semitic / **320**. antiseptic / **321**. antisocial / **322**. anti-terror / **323**. anti-terrorism / **324**. anti-theft / **325**. antithetical / **326**. antitrust / **327**. antiviral / **328**. antivirus / **329**. anti-wrinkle / **330**. anxiety-driven / **331**. anxiety-filled / **332**. anxious / **333**. apathetic / **334**. apathetical / **335**. aphoristic / **336**. aphrodisiac / **337**. apish / **338**. apocalyptic / **339**. apocalyptical / **340**. apocryphal / **341**. apolitical / **342**. apologetic / **343**. apoplectic / **344**. apostolic / **345**. appalled / **346**. appalling / **347**. apparent / **348**. app-based / **349**. app-driven / **350**. appealing / **351**. appellative / **352**. appetizing / **353**. apple-producing / **354**. applicable / **355**. apposite / **356**. appreciable / **357**. appreciative / **358**. apprehensive / **359**. approachable / **360**. appropriate / **361**. approvable / **362**. approving / **363**. approximate / **364**. aquatic / **365**. aqueous / **366**. arabesque / **367**. Arabian / **368**. Arabic / **369**. arable / **370**. arbitrary / **371**. arboreal / **372**. Arcadian / **373**. arcane / **374**. arch / **375**. archaic / **376**. archeological / **377**. architectonic / **378**. architectonical / **379**. architectural / **380**. arctic / **381**. ardent / **382**. arduous / **383**. arguable / **384**. argumentative / **385**. aristocratic / **386**. arithmetical / **387**. armed / **388**. armless / **389**. armorial / **390**. armor-plated / **391**. arm-wrestling / **392**. army-dominated / **393**. army-led / **394**. aromatic / **395**. arrayed / **396**. arrogant / **397**. arsenic-tainted / **398**. arterial / **399**. art-filled / **400**. artful / **401**. arthritic / **402**. articulate / **403**. articulated / **404**. artificial / **405**. artificially ripened / **406**. artistic / **407**. artless / **408**. ascertainable / **409**. ascetic / **410**. ascetical / **411**. ascribable / **412**. aseptic / **413**. asexual /

414. ashamed / 415. ash-emitting / 416. ashen / 417. ash-smeared / 418. Asian / 419. Asiatic / 420. asinine / 421. askew / 422. asleep / 423. aspect-oriented / 424. aspiring / 425. aspirin-induced / 426. assailable / 427. assertive / 428. assessable / 429. assiduous / 430. assignable / 431. assistant / 432. associate / 433. associated / 434. associational / 435. associative / 436. assorted / 437. assumed / 438. assuming / 439. assured / 440. asthmatic / 441. astonished / 442. astonishing / 443. astounded / 444. astounding / 445. astringent / 446. astronomical / 447. astute / 448. asymmetric / 449. asymptomatic / 450. atavistic / 451. ataxic / 452. atheistic / 453. athletic / 454. atmospheric / 455. atomic / 456. atonal / 457. atrocious / 458. attachable / 459. attached / 460. attainable / 461. attempted / 462. attendant / 463. attention-grabbing / 464. attention-seeking / 465. attentive / 466. attenuated / 467. attestable / 468. attitudinal / 469. attractive / 470. attributable / 471. attributive / 472. attritional / 473. attuned / 474. audacious / 475. audible / 476. auditory / 477. august / 478. aural / 479. aureate / 480. auspicious / 481. austere / 482. austral / 483. Australian / 484. authentic / 485. authorial / 486. authoritative / 487. autobiographical / 488. autocratic / 489. autogenic / 490. automatic / 491. autonomous / 492. autumnal / 493. auxiliary / 494. available / 495. avalanche-prone / 496. avaricious / 497. average / 498. avertable / 499. avian / 500. aviation-centric / 501. aviation-related / 502. avid / 503. avoidable / 504. avowed / 505. awake / 506. award-winning / 507. awareness-raising / 508. awash / 509. awe-inspiring / 510. aweless / 511. awesome / 512. awestruck / 513. awful / 514. awkward / 515. awry / 516. axial / 517. axiomatic / 518. azure

02b. <u>Useful</u> <u>Adjectives</u> -- 'B'

1. baby / 2. baby-faced / 3. babyish / 4. bacchanalian / 5. back / 6. back-breaking / 7. back-door / 8. back-end / 9. backhanded / 10. backless / 11. backmost / 12. backstage / 13. backstairs / 14. backstreet / 15. back-to-front / 16. backward / 17. backward-looking / 18. bacteria-infested / 19. bacterial / 20. bacteria-riddled / 21. bad / 22. badass / 23. badly conceived / 24. badly constructed / 25. badly damaged / 26. badly designed / 27. badly framed / 28. badly organized / 29. bad-tempered / 30. baggy / 31. baking / 32. balanced / 33. bald / 34. bald-faced / 35. balding / 36. baleful / 37. balky / 38. balletic / 39. ballistic / 40. balmy / 41. Baltic / 42. banal / 43. bandy / 44. banged up / 45. bankable / 46. bank-driven / 47. bank-owned / 48. bank-related / 49. bankrupt / 50. banqueting / 51. barbaric / 52. barbarous / 53. barbed / 54. bare / 55. bareback / 56. bare-chested / 57. barefaced / 58. barefoot / 59. bare-footed / 60. bareheaded / 61. barely-literate / 62. barmy / 63. barnstorming / 64. barometrical / 65. baronial / 66. barrel-shaped / 67. base / 68. based / 69. baseless / 70. bashful / 71. basic / 72. Basque / 73. bass / 74. bathed / 75. bat-infested / 76. battered / 77. battery-operated / 78. battery-oriented / 79. battery-powered / 80. battle-hardened / 81. battle-scarred / 82. battle-torn / 83. batty / 84. bawdy / 85. beacon-sporting / 86. beaded / 87. beady / 88. beaked / 89. beamed / 90. bearable / 91. beardless / 92. bearish / 93. beatific / 94. beat-up / 95. beauteous / 96. beautiful / 97. beauty conscious / 98. be-calmed / 99. becoming / 100. bed bug-infested / 101. bed-bound / 102. bed-making / 103. bedraggled / 104. bed-ridden / 105. beefy / 106. befuddled / 107. beguiling / 108. belated / 109. beleaguered / 110. believable / 111. belligerent / 112. beloved / 113. below normal / 114. belted / 115. bemused / 116. bendable / 117. bendy / 118. beneficent / 119. beneficial / 120. benevolent / 121. benighted / 122. benign / 123. bereaved / 124. Berliner / 125. berserk / 126. beseeching / 127. besotted / 128. bespectacled / 129. bestial / 130. betrothed / 131. better-equipped / 132. better-paying / 133. beveled / 134. bewigged / 135. bewildering / 136. bewitching / 137. biannual / 138. biased / 139. biblical / 140. bibliographical / 141. bibulous / 142. bicameral / 143. bicoastal / 144. biddable / 145. biennial / 146. big / 147. bigamous / 148. big-brained /

149. big-cheeked / 150. big-haired / 151. big-headed / 152. big-hearted / 153. bigoted / 154. big-ticket / 155. bike-borne / 156. bilateral / 157. bilingual / 158. bilious / 159. billable / 160. bimonthly / 161. binding / 162. bio-based / 163. biodegradable / 164. biological / 165. biomedical / 166. biometric / 167. biometrical / 168. bionic / 169. biotic / 170. biotical / 171. bipartite / 172. bipedal / 173. biracial / 174. bird-shaped / 175. bird-watching / 176. bisexual / 177. bitchy / 178. bite-sized / 179. biting / 180. bitter / 181. bitterly contested / 182. bitter-sweet / 183. bitumen-built / 184. bitumen-topped / 185. bituminous / 186. bizarre / 187. black-clad / 188. black-eyed / 189. black-footed / 190. blamable / 191. blameless / 192. blameworthy / 193. bland / 194. blank / 195. blanket-draped / 196. blasé / 197. blasphemous / 198. blasted / 199. blast-hit / 200. blatant / 201. blazing / 202. bleach-soaked / 203. bleak / 204. bleary / 205. bleary-eyed / 206. bleeding / 207. blessed / 208. blind / 209. blindfold / 210. blinding / 211. blinkered / 212. blinking / 213. blissful / 214. blistering / 215. blithe / 216. blithering / 217. bloated / 218. blonde / 219. blood-borne / 220. blood-curdling / 221. blood-filled / 222. bloodless / 223. blood-red / 224. blood-smeared / 225. blood-soaked / 226. blood-spattered / 227. blood-stained / 228. bloody / 229. bloody-minded / 230. blooming / 231. blotto / 232. blowsy / 233. blue / 234. blue-beaked / 235. blue-blooded / 236. blue-cheeked / 237. blue-chip / 238. blue-clothed / 239. blue-collar / 240. blue-eyed / 241. blue-on-blue / 242. blue-sky / 243. bluesy / 244. Bluetooth-enabled / 245. bluff / 246. bluish / 247. blunt / 248. blurred / 249. blurry / 250. blustery / 251. boastful / 252. bodacious / 253. bodiless / 254. bodily / 255. body-baring / 256. bog-standard / 257. bogus / 258. boisterous / 259. bold / 260. bolt-action / 261. bombed / 262. bomb-fitted / 263. bomb-laden / 264. bomb-making / 265. bombproof / 266. bone dry / 267. bone idle / 268. bone-chilling / 269. boneless / 270. bone-rattling / 271. bonkers / 272. bonny / 273. bony / 274. bookable / 275. bookish / 276. book-smart / 277. boorish / 278. boot-cut / 279. bootleg / 280. bootless / 281. border guarding / 282. border-centric / 283. borderless / 284. bored / 285. boring / 286. boron-deficient / 287. bossy / 288. botanical / 289. bothersome / 290. bottle-green / 291. bottom / 292. bottomed-up / 293. bottomless / 294. bottommost / 295. bouncing / 296. bouncy / 297. bounden / 298. boundless / 299. bounteous / 300. bountiful

/ **301**. bouquet-waving / **302**. bourgeois / **303**. boutique / **304**. bovine / **305**. bowl-shaped / **306**. bow-shaped / **307**. boxed / **308**. box-shaped / **309**. boyish / **310**. bracing / **311**. brackish / **312**. brain-dead / **313**. brainless / **314**. brain-related / **315**. brainy / **316**. brand new / **317**. branded / **318**. brash / **319**. brassy / **320**. brave / **321**. brave-hearted / **322**. brawl-filled / **323**. brawny / **324**. Brazilian / **325**. Brazilian-born / **326**. bread-and-butter / **327**. breakable / **328**. breakaway / **329**. breakneck / **330**. breakthrough / **331**. breathable / **332**. breathless / **333**. breathtaking / **334**. breathy / **335**. breezy / **336**. brick-laden / **337**. brick-throwing / **338**. bridal / **339**. brief / **340**. bright / **341**. bright-eyed / **342**. brilliant / **343**. brimful / **344**. briny / **345**. brisk / **346**. bristly / **347**. British / **348**. British-based / **349**. British-owned / **350**. brittle / **351**. broad / **352**. broad-based / **353**. broad-brush / **354**. broadleaved / **355**. broad-minded / **356**. broad-spectrum / **357**. brocaded / **358**. broke / **359**. broken / **360**. broken heart / **361**. broken-down / **362**. broken-hearted / **363**. bronchial / **364**. bronze / **365**. brooding / **366**. broody / **367**. brotherly / **368**. brown / **369**. brown-eyed / **370**. brownish / **371**. brown-skinned / **372**. bruising / **373**. brusque / **374**. brutal / **375**. brute / **376**. brutish / **377**. bubblegum-flavored / **378**. bubbly / **379**. buccaneering / **380**. bucolic / **381**. bucolical / **382**. budding / **383**. budget / **384**. budgetary / **385**. budget-friendly / **386**. bug-eyed / **387**. buggered / **388**. built-in / **389**. built-up / **390**. bulbous / **391**. bulging / **392**. bulletproof / **393**. bullet-ridden / **394**. bullet-riddled / **395**. bullet-sized / **396**. bullheaded / **397**. bullish / **398**. bull-taming / **399**. bum / **400**. bumbling / **401**. bumper / **402**. bumptious / **403**. bumpy / **404**. buoyant / **405**. burdensome / **406**. bureaucratic / **407**. burial / **408**. burlesque / **409**. burly / **410**. burning / **411**. burnt / **412**. burnt-out / **413**. bushed / **414**. bush-league / **415**. businesslike / **416**. business-to-business / **417**. bust / **418**. busted / **419**. busy / **420**. butch / **421**. butter-smeared / **422**. buttery / **423**. byzantine

1. cabbalistic / 2. cable-stayed / 3. cack-handed / 4. cacophonous / 5. cadaverous / 6. caffeinated / 7. cagey / 8. cake-cutting / 9. calamitous / 10. calcareous / 11. calculable / 12. calculated / 13. callable / 14. callous / 15. callow / 16. callused / 17. calm / 18. calorific / 19. camera-equipped / 20. Canadian-born / 21. cancer-causing / 22. cancerous / 23. cancer-ridden / 24. cancer-stricken / 25. candid / 26. candied / 27. candlelit / 28. can-do / 29. candy-stripped / 30. cane-crushing / 31. cane-growing / 32. canine / 33. canned / 34. cannibalistic / 35. canonical / 36. cantankerous / 37. capable / 38. capacious / 39. capacity-constrained / 40. caparisoned / 41. capital / 42. capital-intensive / 43. capricious / 44. captious / 45. captive / 46. carbon neutral / 47. carbonaceous / 48. carbonated / 49. carboniferous / 50. car-borne / 51. carcinogenic / 52. cardboard / 53. card-carrying / 54. cardinal / 55. cardiovascular / 56. card-issuing / 57. career-oriented / 58. careful / 59. carefully executed / 60. carefully planned / 61. careless / 62. carelessly strewn / 63. caretaker / 64. Caribbean / 65. caring / 66. carnal / 67. carnivorous / 68. carpet-weaving / 69. carroty / 70. carsick / 71. cartilaginous / 72. cartographical / 73. case-sensitive / 74. cash-based / 75. cashed up / 76. cash-laden / 77. cashless / 78. cash-rich / 79. cash-starved / 80. cash-strapped / 81. caste-based / 82. caste-driven / 83. casual / 84. catastrophic / 85. catatonic / 86. catching / 87. catchpenny / 88. catchy / 89. categorical / 90. cathartic / 91. catholic / 92. cattle-grazing / 93. catty / 94. causal / 95. cautionary / 96. cautious / 97. cavalier / 98. cavernous / 99. ceaseless / 100. celebrated / 101. celestial / 102. celibate / 103. cellular / 104. cellulose-based / 105. Cenozoic / 106. censorial / 107. censorious / 108. centennial / 109. centered / 110. central / 111. centrally administered / 112. centrally coordinated / 113. centrally sponsored / 114. centrifugal / 115. centuries-old / 116. ceremonial / 117. ceremonious / 118. certain / 119. certifiable / 120. certificated / 121. certificate-issuing / 122. cerulean / 123. cervical / 124. cetacean / 125. chalky / 126. challenged / 127. challenging / 128. chance / 129. changeable / 130. changeless / 131. chaotic / 132. chapped / 133. character-driven / 134. characteristic / 135. characterless / 136. chargeable / 137. charged / 138. charismatic / 139. charitable / 140.

charming / **141**. charmless / **142**. charred / **143**. chartered / **144**. chart-topping / **145**. chary / **146**. chaste / **147**. chatty / **148**. cheating-free / **149**. checked / **150**. check-related / **151**. cheerful / **152**. cheerless / **153**. cheery / **154**. cheese-paring / **155**. cheesy / **156**. chemical / **157**. chemical-filled / **158**. chemotherapeutical / **159**. cherry / **160**. chest-deep / **161**. chewable / **162**. chicken / **163**. chicken-hearted / **164**. chief / **165**. childish / **166**. childless / **167**. childlike / **168**. childproof / **169**. chill / **170**. chilled / **171**. chilling / **172**. chilly / **173**. Chinese / **174**. chinless / **175**. chintzy / **176**. chipper / **177**. chirpy / **178**. chiseled / **179**. chivalrous / **180**. chockfull / **181**. choice / **182**. choked / **183**. choleric / **184**. choosy / **185**. choppy / **186**. choral / **187**. choreographic / **188**. Christian / **189**. Christmassy / **190**. chromatographic / **191**. chronic / **192**. chronological / **193**. chronometrical / **194**. chubby / **195**. chuffing / **196**. chummy / **197**. chunky / **198**. chunky-cheeked / **199**. churlish / **200**. cine / **201**. cinematic / **202**. cinematographic / **203**. circuitous / **204**. circular / **205**. circulatory / **206**. circumferential / **207**. circumlocutory / **208**. circumspect / **209**. circumstantial / **210**. citified / **211**. citizen-centric / **212**. citizen-driven / **213**. citric / **214**. civic / **215**. civil / **216**. civilian / **217**. civilized / **218**. clad / **219**. claimable / **220**. clairvoyant / **221**. clammy / **222**. clamorous / **223**. clannish / **224**. clapped out / **225**. classic / **226**. classical / **227**. classifiable / **228**. classified / **229**. classless / **230**. classy / **231**. claustrophobic / **232**. clean / **233**. clean-cut / **234**. clean-limbed / **235**. cleanliness-oriented / **236**. cleanliness-related / **237**. clean-living / **238**. clean-shaven / **239**. clear / **240**. clear-cut / **241**. clear-headed / **242**. clear-sighted / **243**. cleft / **244**. clement / **245**. clerical / **246**. clever / **247**. clickable / **248**. climactic / **249**. climate-resilient / **250**. climbable / **251**. clinical / **252**. cloistered / **253**. closable / **254**. close / **255**. close-cropped / **256**. closed / **257**. closed-captioned / **258**. close-knit / **259**. closely contested / **260**. closely guarded / **261**. close-mouthed / **262**. close-range / **263**. close-run / **264**. close-set / **265**. closing / **266**. cloth-eared / **267**. clothed / **268**. cloud-based / **269**. cloudless / **270**. cloudy / **271**. clownish / **272**. cloying / **273**. clucky / **274**. clued-up / **275**. clueless / **276**. clumpy / **277**. clumsy / **278**. clunky / **279**. cluttered / **280**. coal-fired / **281**. coal-laden / **282**. coal-powered / **283**. coarse / **284**. coastal / **285**. cobweb-draped / **286**. cock-a-hoop / **287**. cockamamie / **288**. cockeyed / **289**. cockroach-infested / **290**. cocksure / **291**. cocky / **292**. coconut-flavored / **293**. cod / **294**. coded / **295**. co-educational / **296**. coercible / **297**. coercive / **298**. coffee-stained / **299**. coffin-encased / **300**. cogent / **301**. cognate / **302**. cognitive / **303**. cognizant / **304**. coherent / **305**. cohesive / **306**. coincident / **307**. coincidental / **308**. cola-flavored / **309**. cold / **310**. cold-adapted / **311**. cold-blooded / **312**. cold-hearted / **313**. cold-related / **314**. collaborative / **315**. collagen-induced / **316**. collapsible / **317**. collarless / **318**. collateral / **319**. collectable / **320**. collected / **321**. collectible / **322**. collective / **323**. collegial / **324**. colloquial / **325**. collusive / **326**. colonial / **327**. colonic / **328**. colored / **329**. colorless / **330**. color-throwing / **331**. combative / **332**. combinational / **333**. combustible / **334**. comely / **335**. comestible / **336**. comfortable / **337**. comforting / **338**. comfy / **339**. comic / **340**. comical / **341**. coming / **342**. commanding / **343**. commemorational / **344**. commendable / **345**. commensurate / **346**. commerce-related / **347**. commercial / **348**. commercially sold / **349**. commercially viable / **350**. committed / **351**. commodity-centric / **352**. commodity-oriented / **353**. common / **354**. commonly used / **355**. communal / **356**. communally charged / **357**. communally troubled / **358**. communally volatile / **359**. communally-sensitive / **360**. communicable / **361**. communicational / **362**. communicative / **363**. community-owned / **364**. commutative / **365**. compact / **366**. companionable / **367**. comparable / **368**. comparative / **369**. compassionate / **370**. compatible / **371**. compelling / **372**. compendious / **373**. competent / **374**. competitive / **375**. complacent / **376**. complaint-driven / **377**. complaisant / **378**. complete / **379**. complex / **380**. compliable / **381**. compliant / **382**. complicated / **383**. complicit / **384**. complimentary / **385**. composed / **386**. composite / **387**. compositional / **388**. compound / **389**. comprehensible / **390**. comprehensive / **391**. compressible / **392**. compromising / **393**. compulsive / **394**. compulsory / **395**. computable / **396**. computational / **397**. computer-based / **398**. computer-controlled / **399**. conceited / **400**. conceivable / **401**. concentrated / **402**. concentric / **403**. conceptual / **404**. concerned / **405**. concerted / **406**. concessionary / **407**. concessive / **408**. conciliatory / **409**. concise / **410**. conclusive / **411**. concomitant / **412**. concurrent / **413**. condemnable / **414**. condescending / **415**. condign / **416**. conditional / **417**. condition-based / **418**. condonable / **419**. conducive / **420**. conductional / **421**. conductive / **422**. cone-shaped / **423**.

confederate / **424**. conferential / **425**. confidence-building / **426**. confident / **427**. confidential / **428**. confiding / **429**. configurable / **430**. confined / **431**. confirmative / **432**. confirmed / **433**. conflicted / **434**. conflict-hit / **435**. conflict-ridden / **436**. conformable / **437**. confrontational / **438**. confusable / **439**. confused / **440**. confusing / **441**. congenial / **442**. congenital / **443**. congested / **444**. congratulatory / **445**. congress-ruled / **446**. congruent / **447**. conical / **448**. coniferous / **449**. conjoint / **450**. conjugal / **451**. connected / **452**. connectionless / **453**. connective / **454**. conniving / **455**. connubial / **456**. conquerable / **457**. consanguineous / **458**. conscientious / **459**. conscious / **460**. consecutive / **461**. consensual / **462**. consequential / **463**. conservative / **464**. considerable / **465**. considerate / **466**. consistent / **467**. consolatory / **468**. consonant / **469**. conspicuous / **470**. conspiratorial / **471**. constant / **472**. constipated / **473**. constitutional / **474**. constitutive / **475**. constrained / **476**. constructible / **477**. constructional / **478**. construction-allied / **479**. constructive / **480**. consultative / **481**. consumable / **482**. consumer-centric / **483**. consumer-friendly / **484**. consumer-oriented / **485**. consuming / **486**. consumptive / **487**. contactable / **488**. contagious / **489**. containable / **490**. containerized / **491**. contemplative / **492**. contemporaneous / **493**. contemporary / **494**. contemptible / **495**. contemptuous / **496**. content-driven / **497**. contented / **498**. contentious / **499**. contestable / **500**. contextual / **501**. contiguous / **502**. continental / **503**. contingent / **504**. continual / **505**. continuous / **506**. contoured / **507**. contractible / **508**. contractile / **509**. contractual / **510**. contradictory / **511**. contrapuntal / **512**. contrary / **513**. contrasting / **514**. contrastive / **515**. contributory / **516**. contrite / **517**. contrived / **518**. controllable / **519**. controlled / **520**. controversial / **521**. controversy-generating / **522**. controversy-hit / **523**. controversy-marred / **524**. controversy-ridden / **525**. contumacious / **526**. conventional / **527**. conversant / **528**. conversational / **529**. convertible / **530**. convinced / **531**. convivial / **532**. convoluted / **533**. convulsive / **534**. cookie-cutter / **535**. cooking / **536**. cool / **537**. cool-headed / **538**. co-operative / **539**. copious / **540**. copper-bottomed / **541**. coppery / **542**. copybook / **543**. copycat / **544**. copyrightable / **545**. corded / **546**. cordial / **547**. cordless / **548** coronary / **549**. corporeal / **550**. corpulent / **551**. correct / **552**. correctable / **553**. correctional / **554**. corrective / **555**. corresponding / **556**.

corroborative / **557**. corrosive / **558**. corrugated / **559**. corruptible / **560**. corruption-driven / **561**. corruption-free / **562**. corruption-plagued / **563**. corruption-prone / **564**. corruption-tainted / **565**. cosmetic / **566**. cosmopolitan / **567**. cost-cutting / **568**. cost-effective / **569**. costless / **570**. costumed / **571**. coterminous / **572**. countable / **573**. counterfactual / **574**. counterfeit / **575**. counter-insurgency / **576**. counter-intuitive / **577**. counter-militancy / **578**. counter-terrorism / **579**. countless / **580**. country-made / **581**. courageous / **582**. courteous / **583**. courtesy / **584**. court-inspired / **585**. court-mandated / **586**. court-ordered / **587**. court-referred / **588**. court-room / **589**. covered / **590**. covetous / **591**. cozy / **592**. crabbed / **593**. crabby / **594**. crabwise / **595**. crackbrained / **596**. cracked / **597**. cracking / **598**. crafty / **599**. craggy / **600**. crammed / **601**. cramped / **602**. cranky / **603**. crappy / **604**. crash / **605**. crash-like / **606**. crash-marred / **607**. crass / **608**. craven / **609**. crazed / **610**. crazy / **611**. creaky / **612**. cream / **613**. creamy / **614**. creatable / **615**. creational / **616**. creative / **617**. credible / **618**. creditable / **619**. creditworthy / **620**. credulous / **621**. creepy / **622**. crepuscular / **623**. crested / **624**. crestfallen / **625**. cretaceous / **626**. cricket-betting / **627**. crime-ridden / **628**. cringe-worthy / **629**. crinkly / **630**. crisis-hit / **631**. crisis-like / **632**. crisis-ridden / **633**. crisp / **634**. critical / **635**. critically ill / **636**. critically injured / **637**. croaky / **638**. crocked / **639**. crocodile-infested / **640**. crook / **641**. crooked / **642**. crop-based / **643**. cross-border / **644**. cross-country / **645**. cross-cultural / **646**. cross-curricular / **647**. cross-eyed / **648**. cross-legged / **649**. cross-market / **650**. cross-platform / **651**. cross-species / **652**. cross-voting / **653**. crowd-pulling / **654**. crowd-sourced / **655**. crucial / **656**. crucible / **657**. cruddy / **658**. crude / **659**. cruel / **660**. crummy / **661**. crunch / **662**. crunchy / **663**. crushing / **664**. crusted / **665**. crusty / **666**. crying / **667**. cryogenic / **668**. cryptic / **669**. crystal-clear / **670**. crystallized / **671**. cryptozoic / **672**. Cuban / **673**. cube-shaped / **674**. cubic / **675**. cubical / **676**. cuckoo / **677**. cuddly / **678**. culpable / **679**. cult / **680**. cultivable / **681**. cultivated / **682**. cultural / **683**. cultured / **684**. culture-driven / **685**. cumbersome / **686**. cumulative / **687**. cunning / **688**. curable / **689**. curative / **690**. curatorial / **691**. curfew-like / **692**. curious / **693**. curly / **694**. curly-haired / **695**. current / **696**. curried / **697**. cursed / **698**. cursive / **699**. cursory / **700**. curt / **701**. curvaceous / **702**. curvilinear / **703**. cushy / **704**. cussed / **705**.

custodial / **706**. custom / **707**. customary / **708**. custom-built / **709**. customer-centric / **710**. customizable / **711**. custom-made / **712**. cute / **713**. cut-off / **714**. cut-price / **715**. cut-throat / **716**. cutting / **717**. cutting-edge / **718**. cybernetic / **719**. cyclic / **720**. cyclical / **721**. cyclone-affected / **722**. cylindrical / **723**. cynical

<u>02d.</u> <u>Useful</u> <u>Adjectives</u> -- 'D'

1. dacoit-infested / **2**. dacoit-prone / **3**. daffy / **4**. daft / **5**. daily / **6**. dainty / **7**. dairy / **8**. dairy-based / **9**. damaging / **10**. damn / **11**. damnable / **12**. damned / **13**. damnedest / **14**. damning / **15**. danceable / **16**. dance-centric / **17**. dandified / **18**. dandy / **19**. dang / **20**. dangerous / **21**. Danish / **22**. dank / **23**. dappled / **24**. daring / **25**. dark / **26**. dark-haired / **27**. darkling / **28**. darkness-filled / **29**. dark-skinned / **30**. dark-tinted / **31**. darn / **32**. dashed / **33**. data-centric / **34**. dauntless / **35**. daylong / **36**. day-long / **37**. day-time / **38**. day-to-day / **39**. dead beat / **40**. deadly / **41**. deaf / **42**. deafening / **43**. dear / **44**. death-related / **45**. debatable / **46**. debauched / **47**. debonair / **48**. debris-laden / **49**. debt-crippled / **50**. debt-laden / **51**. debt-ridden / **52**. debt-trapped / **53**. decadent / **54**. decade-old / **55**. decades-long / **56**. decaffeinated / **57**. deceased / **58**. deceitful / **59**. deceptive / **60**. decidable / **61**. decided / **62**. deciduous / **63**. decimal / **64**. decipherable / **65**. decisive / **66**. declarable / **67**. declared / **68**. decomposable / **69**. decorative / **70**. decorous / **71**. decrepit / **72**. dedicated / **73**. deducible / **74**. deductible / **75**. deductive / **76**. deep / **77**. deeply conservative / **78**. deeply divided / **79**. deeply held / **80**. deeply ingrained / **81**. deeply rooted / **82**. deeply shameful / **83**. deeply wooded / **84**. deeply worrying / **85**. deep-lying / **86**. deep-rooted / **87**. deep-seated / **88**. deep-set / **89**. deep-throated / **90**. defamatory / **91**. defective / **92**. defendable / **93**. defenseless / **94**. defense-related / **95**. defensible / **96**. defensive / **97**. defensive-oriented / **98**. deferential / **99**. defiant / **100**. deficient / **101**. definable / **102**. defining / **103**. definite / **104**. definitive / **105**. deflectable / **106**. deformable / **107**. deformational / **108**. deformed / **109**. deft / **110**. deftly executed / **111**. defunct / **112**. degenerative / **113**. degradable / **114**. degrading / **115**. dehydrated / **116**. dehydration-related / **117**. deictic / **118**. dejected / **119**. delectable / **120**. deliberate / **121**. delicate / **122**. delicious / **123**. delighted / **124**. delightful / **125**. delinquent / **126**. delirious / **127**. deliverable / **128**. delusive / **129**. demagogic / **130**. demand-based / **131**. demand-driven / **132**. demanding / **133**. demeaning / **134**. demented / **135**. dementia-stricken / **136**. democrat-dominated / **137**. democratic / **138**. demographic / **139**. demographical / **140**. demonic / **141**. demonical / **142**. demon-infested / **143**. demonstrable / **144**.

demonstrative / **145**. demotic / **146**. demountable / **147**. dengue-causing / **148**. deniable / **149**. denial / **150**. denominational / **151**. dense / **152**. densely populated / **153**. dental / **154**. departed / **155**. departmental / **156**. dependable / **157**. dependent / **158**. deplorable / **159**. depositional / **160**. depraved / **161**. depressed / **162**. depressing / **163**. depressive / **164**. deprived / **165**. deranged / **166**. derelict / **167**. derisive / **168**. derisory / **169**. derivable / **170**. derivative / **171**. derogatory / **172**. describable / **173**. descriptive / **174**. deserted / **175**. deserving / **176**. desiccated / **177**. designable / **178**. designate / **179**. designer / **180**. design-oriented / **181**. desirable / **182**. desire-based / **183**. desirous / **184**. desolate / **185**. despairing / **186**. desperate / **187**. despicable / **188**. despondent / **189**. destination / **190**. destined / **191**. destitute / **192**. destroyable / **193**. destructive / **194**. desultory / **195**. detachable / **196**. detached / **197**. detailed / **198**. detectable / **199**. determinable / **200**. determinate / **201**. determined / **202**. detestable / **203**. detrimental / **204**. deuced / **205**. devastated / **206**. devastating / **207**. developed / **208**. developing / **209**. developmental / **210**. deviant / **211**. device-centric / **212**. deviled / **213**. devilish / **214**. devious / **215**. devoid / **216**. devolved / **217**. devoted / **218**. devotional / **219**. devout / **220**. dewy-eyed / **221**. dexterous / **222**. diabetic / **223**. diabolic / **224**. diabolical / **225**. diachronic / **226**. diagnosable / **227**. diagnostic / **228**. diagonal / **229**. diagrammatic / **230**. dialectical / **231**. diamantine / **232**. diametrical / **233**. diamond-encrusted / **234**. diamond-shaped / **235**. diaphanous / **236**. Diaspora-related / **237**. diatomic / **238**. diatonic / **239**. dicey / **240**. dichotomous / **241**. dictator-controlled / **242**. dictatorial / **243**. didactic / **244**. didactical / **245**. die-cast / **246**. diehard / **247**. diesel-guzzling / **248**. diesel-operated / **249**. diesel-powered / **250**. diesel-run / **251**. diet-conscious / **252**. diet-induced / **253**. diet-related / **254**. different / **255**. differentiable / **256**. differential / **257**. difficult-to-reach / **258**. diffident / **259**. diffuse / **260**. digestible / **261**. digestive / **262**. digital / **263**. digitally-illiterate / **264**. dignified / **265**. dilapidated / **266**. dilatable / **267**. dilatory / **268**. diligent / **269**. dilute / **270**. dim / **271**. dimensionless / **272**. diminishable / **273**. diminutive / **274**. dimly lit / **275**. dimple-cheeked / **276**. dingy / **277**. dinky / **278**. diploid / **279**. diplomatic / **280**. dippy / **281**. dire / **282**. direct / **283**. directional / **284**. directionless / **285**. directive / **286**. directorial / **287**. dirigible / **288**. dirt cheap / **289**. dirt-laden / **290**. dirt-smeared / **291**. dirty / **292**. disabled / **293**. disadvantaged / **294**. disadvantageous / **295**. disaffected / **296**. disagreeable / **297**. disappointed / **298**. disapproving / **299**. disarming / **300**. disaster-prone / **301**. disaster-stricken / **302**. disastrous / **303**. discernible / **304**. discerning / **305**. disciplinary / **306**. disconcerting / **307**. disconnected / **308**. disconsolate / **309**. discontented / **310**. discontinuous / **311**. discordant / **312**. discountable / **313**. discourteous / **314**. discoverable / **315**. discreditable / **316**. discrete / **317**. discretional / **318**. discretionary / **319**. discriminating / **320**. discriminatory / **321**. disc-shaped / **322**. discussable / **323**. disdainful / **324**. disease-afflicted / **325**. diseased / **326**. disease-free / **327**. disease-ridden / **328**. disease-stricken / **329**. disembodied / **330**. disenchanted / **331**. disgraceful / **332**. disgruntled / **333**. disgusted / **334**. disgusting / **335**. disheveled / **336**. dishonorable / **337**. disillusioned / **338**. disinclined / **339**. disingenuous / **340**. disinterested / **341**. disjointed / **342**. disloyal / **343**. dismal / **344**. dismayed / **345**. dismissible / **346**. dismissive / **347**. disobedient / **348**. disobliging / **349**. disordered / **350**. disorganized / **351**. dispassionate / **352**. dispensable / **353**. dispirited / **354**. displayable / **355**. displeased / **356**. disposable / **357**. disposed / **358**. disproportionate / **359**. disprovable / **360**. disputable / **361**. disquieting / **362**. disreputable / **363**. disrespectful / **364**. disruptive / **365**. dissatisfied / **366**. dissenting / **367**. dissertational / **368**. dissident / **369**. dissipated / **370**. dissolute / **371**. distal / **372**. distant / **373**. distasteful / **374**. distinct / **375**. distinctive / **376**. distinguishable / **377**. distinguished / **378**. distracted / **379**. distraught / **380**. distressed / **381**. distressing / **382**. distributable / **383**. distributional / **384**. distributive / **385**. district-based / **386**. disturbed / **387**. disturbing / **388**. disused / **389**. ditzy / **390**. diurnal / **391**. diverse / **392**. diversionary / **393**. diverting / **394**. divided / **395**. divine / **396**. divisible / **397**. divisional / **398**. divisive / **399**. divorced / **400**. dizzy / **401**. dizzying / **402**. doable / **403**. docile / **404**. doctoral / **405**. doctor-led / **406**. doctrinal / **407**. documentary / **408**. doddering / **409**. dodgy / **410**. doe-eyed / **411**. dog-eared / **412**. dogged / **413**. doggone / **414**. dogmatic / **415**. dog-tired / **416**. dog-tracking / **417**. doleful / **418**. dolorous / **419**. domestic / **420**. domesticated / **421**. domiciled / **422**. domiciliary / **423**. domineering / **424**. donnish / **425**. doom-laden / **426**. do-or-die / **427**. dope-free / **428**. dopey / **429**. dormant / **430**. dorsal / **431**. dotted / **432**. dotty / **433**. double / **434**.

double-action / **435**. double-blind / **436**. double-edged / **437**. double-faced / **438**. double-glazed / **439**. double-humped / **440**. double-jointed / **441**. double-quick / **442**. doubtful / **443**. doubtless / **444**. doughty / **445**. dovish / **446**. dowdy / **447**. down / **448**. down and out / **449**. down to earth / **450**. downbeat / **451**. downcast / **452**. downhearted / **453**. downhill / **454**. downright / **455**. downscale / **456**. downstream / **457**. downtrodden / **458**. downward / **459**. downy / **460**. dozy / **461**. drab / **462**. draconian / **463**. drain-cleaning / **464**. drained / **465**. drama-filled / **466**. dramatic / **467**. drastic / **468**. Dravidian / **469**. drawn / **470**. dread / **471**. dreaded / **472**. dreadful / **473**. dreamless / **474**. dreamlike / **475**. dreamy / **476**. dreary / **477**. dressed / **478**. dressy / **479**. drinkable / **480**. dripping / **481**. drippy / **482**. drivable / **483**. driven / **484**. driverless / **485**. driving / **486**. droll / **487**. droopy / **488**. drop-in / **489**. drought-afflicted / **490**. drought-hit / **491**. drought-like / **492**. drought-prone / **493**. drought-stricken / **494**. drowsy / **495**. druggy / **496**. drug-induced / **497**. drug-related / **498**. drug-resistant / **499**. drunken / **500**. dry / **501**. dry-roasted / **502**. dual-purpose / **503**. dubious / **504**. ducky / **505**. ductile / **506**. dud / **507**. due / **508**. duff / **509**. dulcet / **510**. dull / **511**. dull-witted / **512**. dumb / **513**. dumbfounded / **514**. dumbstruck / **515**. dummy / **516**. dumpy / **517**. duplicate / **518**. duplicitous / **519**. durable / **520**. durative / **521**. dusky / **522**. dusky-cheeked / **523**. dust-laden / **524**. dusty / **525**. dutiful / **526**. duty-bound / **527**. duty-free / **528**. dwarf / **529**. dying / **530**. dynamic / **531**. dynamical / **532**. dynastic / **533**. dyspeptic

02e. Useful Adjectives -- 'E'

1. eager / 2. eagle-eyed / 3. earnest / 4. earnings-related / 5. ear-piercing / 6. ear-shattering / 7. earth-like / 8. earthy / 9. easeful / 10. easily accessible / 11. east / 12. easterly / 13. eastern / 14. easternmost / 15. easy / 16. easy-care / 17. easy-going / 18. easy-to-understand / 19. eatable / 20. ebony / 21. ebullient / 22. eccentric / 23. ecclesiastical / 24. eclectic / 25. eco-friendly / 26. eco-friendly / 27. ecologically conscious / 28. ecologically crucial / 29. ecologically fragile/sensitive / 30. econometrical / 31. economic / 32. economical / 33. economically deprived / 34. eco-saving / 35. ecstatic / 36. ecumenical / 37. edgeless / 38. edgy / 39. edible / 40. edifying / 41. editable / 42. editorial / 43. educated / 44. educational / 45. education-based / 46. educative / 47. eel-flavored / 48. eerie / 49. effective / 50. effectual / 51. effeminate / 52. effervescent / 53. effete / 54. efficacious / 55. efficient / 56. effluent-contaminated / 57. effortless / 58. effulgent / 59. effusive / 60. egalitarian / 61. egg-shaped / 62. egg-sized / 63. egocentric / 64. ego-driven / 65. egoistical / 66. egregious / 67. Egyptian-born / 68. Egyptian-led / 69. elaborate / 70. elastic / 71. elated / 72. eldritch / 73. elect / 74. electable / 75. election-bound / 76. election-oriented / 77. election-related / 78. elective / 79. electoral / 80. electrically driven / 81. electricity producing / 82. electric-powered / 83. electrifying / 84. electromagnetic / 85. electronic / 86. electrostatic / 87. elegant / 88. elegiac / 89. elemental / 90. elementary / 91. elephantine / 92. elevated / 93. elevating / 94. elfin / 95. eligible / 96. elliptic / 97. elliptical / 98. elongated / 99. eloquent / 100. elusive / 101. elysian / 102. emaciated / 103. emancipated / 104. embarrassed / 105. embarrassing / 106. embattled / 107. embeddable / 108. emblematic / 109. emblematical / 110. embryological / 111. embryonic / 112. emergent / 113. emeritus / 114. eminent / 115. emission-free / 116. emollient / 117. emotional / 118. emotionally charged / 119. emotionless / 120. emphatic / 121. empirical / 122. employable / 123. empty / 124. empty-handed / 125. empty-headed / 126. enamored / 127. enchanted / 128. enchanting / 129. enclosed / 130. encrusted / 131. encyclopedic / 132. endearing / 133. endemic / 134. endless / 135. endogenous / 136. endothermic / 137. endurable / 138. enduring / 139.

enemy-controlled / **140**. energetic / **141**. energy-related / **142**. energy-rich / **143**. enforceable / **144**. enforced / **145**. engaged / **146**. engaging / **147**. English / **148**. English-speaking / **149**. engrossed / **150**. enhanced / **151**. enigmatic / **152**. enigmatical / **153**. enjoyable / **154**. enlarged / **155**. enlightened / **156**. enlightening / **157**. enlisted / **158**. enormous / **159**. enquiring / **160**. enraptured / **161**. enterprising / **162**. entertaining / **163**. enthusiastic / **164**. enticing / **165**. entire / **166**. entomological / **167**. entrepreneur-driven / **168**. entrepreneur-friendly / **169**. entrepreneurial / **170**. entropic / **171**. enumerable / **172**. enviable / **173**. envious / **174**. environmental-friendly / **175**. environmentally conscious / **176**. ephemeral / **177**. epicene / **178**. epicurean / **179**. epidemic / **180**. epidemical / **181**. epileptic / **182**. Episcopal / **183**. episodic / **184**. epistemic / **185**. epistolary / **186**. epithetical / **187**. epoch-making / **188**. eponymous / **189**. equable / **190**. equal / **191**. equatorial / **192**. equestrian / **193**. equidistant / **194**. equinoctial / **195**. equitable / **196**. equivalent / **197**. equivocal / **198**. erasable / **199**. erectile / **200**. ergative / **201**. ergonomic / **202**. ergonomically designed / **203**. erogenous / **204**. errant / **205**. erroneous / **206**. error-prone / **207**. error-ridden / **208**. erstwhile / **209**. erudite / **210**. eruptive / **211**. escapable / **212**. escaped / **213**. esoteric / **214**. especial / **215**. essential / **216**. essentials-filled / **217**. established / **218**. esthetical / **219**. estimable / **220**. estranged / **221**. eternal / **222**. ethereal / **223**. ethical / **224**. ethnic / **225**. ethnical / **226**. ethnocentric / **227**. ethnographic / **228**. ethnographical / **229**. ethnological / **230**. etiolated / **231**. eugenic / **232**. euphemistic / **233**. euphemistical / **234**. euphonious / **235**. Eurasian / **236**. Eurocentric / **237**. euro-dominated / **238**. European / **239**. evadable / **240**. evaluable / **241**. evaluative / **242**. evangelical / **243**. evasive / **244**. evectional / **245**. even / **246**. evenhanded / **247**. even-handed / **248**. event-driven / **249**. even-tempered / **250**. eventful / **251**. eventual / **252**. ever-ageing / **253**. ever-bustling / **254**. ever-growing / **255**. everlasting / **256**. ever-placid / **257**. ever-strengthening / **258**. ever-worsening / **259**. everyday / **260**. evidence-based / **261**. evidence-gathering / **262**. evidence-tampering / **263**. evident / **264**. evidential / **265**. evil / **266**. evocative / **267**. evolutionary / **268**. exact / **269**. exacting / **270**. exaggerated / **271**. exalted / **272**. examinable / **273**. examinational / **274**. exam-oriented / **275**. exasperated / **276**. exasperating / **277**. excellent /

278. exceptionable / **279**. exceptional / **280**. excess / **281**. excessive / **282**. exchangeable / **283**. excitable / **284**. excited / **285**. exciting / **286**. exclamatory / **287**. exclusionary / **288**. exclusive / **289**. excretory / **290**. excruciating / **291**. excusable / **292**. execrable / **293**. executable / **294**. executive / **295**. exemplary / **296**. exempt / **297**. exercisable / **298**. exercise-induced / **299**. exhausted / **300**. exhausted-looking / **301**. exhaustible / **302**. exhausting / **303**. exhaustive / **304**. exhilarating / **305**. exiguous / **306**. existent / **307**. existential / **308**. existing / **309**. exocrine / **310**. exogenous / **311**. exorbitant / **312**. exothermic / **313**. exotic / **314**. expandable / **315**. expansible / **316**. expansionary / **317**. expansive / **318**. expatriate / **319**. expectant / **320**. expectative / **321**. expected / **322**. expedient / **323**. expeditious / **324**. expendable / **325**. expensive / **326**. expensive-looking / **327**. experienced / **328**. experiential / **329**. experimental / **330**. expert / **331**. explainable / **332**. explanatory / **333**. expletive-filled / **334**. expletive-laden / **335**. explicable / **336**. exploded / **337**. exploitable / **338**. exploitative / **339**. exploratory / **340**. explosion-affected / **341**. explosion-like / **342**. explosive / **343**. explosive-filled / **344**. explosive-packed / **345**. explosive-ridden / **346**. explosive-sniffing / **347**. explosives-packed / **348**. explosives-rigged / **349**. exponential / **350**. exportable / **351**. export-driven / **352**. export-oriented / **353**. exposable / **354**. exposed / **355**. expository / **356**. express / **357**. expressible / **358**. expressionless / **359**. expressive / **360**. exquisite / **361**. extant / **362**. extempore / **363**. extendable / **364**. extended / **365**. extendible / **366**. extensible / **367**. extensive / **368**. extenuating / **369**. exterior / **370**. external / **371**. externally oriented / **372**. extortionate / **373**. extracellular / **374**. extracorporeal / **375**. extractable / **376**. extractive / **377**. extracurricular / **378**. extraditable / **379**. extragalactic / **380**. extrajudicial / **381**. extra-long / **382**. extramarital / **383**. extramural / **384**. extraneous / **385**. extraordinaire / **386**. extraordinarily / **387**. extraordinary / **388**. extrapolate / **389**. extrapolation / **390**. extra-sensory / **391**. extra-solar / **392**. extra-special / **393**. extraterrestrial / **394**. extraterritorial / **395**. extra-thin / **396**. extravagance / **397**. extravagant / **398**. extravaganza / **399**. extreme / **400**. extremism-hit / **401**. extrinsic / **402**. extroverted / **403**. extrusive / **404**. exultant / **405**. eyeless

02f. <u>Useful</u> <u>Adjectives</u> -- 'F'

1. fabled / 2. fabulous / 3. face-covering / 4. faceless / 5. face-saving / 6. facetious / 7. face-to-face / 8. facial / 9. fact-finding / 10. factional / 11. faction-ridden / 12. factious / 13. factitious / 14. factorial / 15. factory-based / 16. factory-built / 17. factory-made / 18. factual / 19. factually incorrect / 20. faddy / 21. fagged / 22. failed / 23. fail-safe / 24. faint / 25. faint-hearted / 26. fair / 27. fair-haired / 28. fair-minded / 29. fair-trade / 30. fair-weather / 31. fairy-tale / 32. faith-based / 33. faithful / 34. faithless / 35. faith-related / 36. fake / 37. fallacious / 38. fallen / 39. fallible / 40. fallow / 41. false / 42. falsifiable / 43. famed / 44. fame-obsessed / 45. familial / 46. familiar / 47. family / 48. family-centric / 49. family-oriented / 50. family-owned / 51. famine-affected / 52. famine-hit / 53. famished / 54. famous / 55. fanatical / 56. fanciful / 57. fancy-free / 58. fantastic / 59. fantastical / 60. far / 61. faraway / 62. farcical / 63. far-fetched / 64. far-flung / 65. farmer-friendly / 66. far-reaching / 67. far-sighted / 68. fascinated / 69. fascinating / 70. fashionable / 71. fashion-conscious / 72. fashion-forward / 73. fast / 74. fast-acting / 75. fast-changing / 76. fast-developing / 77. fast-dying / 78. fast-fading / 79. fast-fashion / 80. fast-food / 81. fast-growing / 82. fastidious / 83. fast-melting / 84. fast-moving / 85. fast-paced / 86. fast-receding / 87. fast-shrinking / 88. fast-track / 89. fat / 90. fatal / 91. fatalistic / 92. fated / 93. fateful / 94. fathomless / 95. fatigue related / 96. fatigued / 97. fatigue-reducing / 98. fatless / 99. fattening / 100. fatty / 101. fatuous / 102. faultless / 103. faulty / 104. Faustian / 105. faux / 106. favorable / 107. favored / 108. favorite / 109. fawn / 110. fear-driven / 111. fearful / 112. fearless / 113. fearsome / 114. fearsome-looking / 115. fear-stricken / 116. fear-struck / 117. feasible / 118. feather-bedecked / 119. feather-brained / 120. feathered / 121. feathery / 122. feature-length / 123. featureless / 124. feature-rich / 125. febrile / 126. feckless / 127. fecund / 128. federal / 129. feeble / 130. feeble-minded / 131. feeder / 132. feel-good / 133. felicitous / 134. feline / 135. fellow / 136. felonious / 137. female / 138. female-dominated / 139. female-oriented / 140. feminine / 141. ferocious / 142. ferrous / 143. fertile / 144. fervent / 145. fervid / 146. festive / 147. fetal / 148. fetching / 149. fetid / 150. feudal / 151. feudalistic / 152. fevered / 153. feverish / 154. few

/ **155**. fey / **156**. fibrous / **157**. fickle / **158**. fictional / **159**. fictitious / **160**. fiddling / **161**. fidgety / **162**. fiduciary / **163**. fiendish / **164**. fierce / **165**. fifty-fifty / **166**. figured / **167**. filamentous / **168**. filial / **169**. Filipino / **170**. filling / **171**. filmic / **172**. filth-laden / **173**. filthy / **174**. final / **175**. financial / **176**. financially distressed / **177**. financially strained / **178**. findable / **179**. fine / **180**. fine-looking / **181**. finely-honed / **182**. fingerless / **183**. finicky / **184**. finished / **185**. finite / **186**. Finnish / **187**. firearm-related / **188**. fire-caused / **189**. firecracker-manufacturing / **190**. fire-fighting / **191**. fire-resistant / **192**. firm / **193**. firstborn / **194**. first-class / **195**. first-degree / **196**. first-ever / **197**. first-hand / **198**. first-rate / **199**. first-time / **200**. fiscal / **201**. fishy / **202**. fit / **203**. fitful / **204**. fitted / **205**. fitting / **206**. five-dimensional / **207**. five-fold / **208**. five-star / **209**. fixable / **210**. fixated / **211**. fixed / **212**. fixed-term / **213**. fixed-wing / **214**. fizzy / **215**. flabbergasted / **216**. flaccid / **217**. flag hoisting / **218**. flag-bearer / **219**. flag-draped / **220**. flagged / **221**. flag-lowering / **222**. flags-fitted / **223**. flag-waving / **224**. flaky / **225**. flamboyant / **226**. flameproof / **227**. flaming / **228**. flammable / **229**. flappable / **230**. flared / **231**. flash / **232**. flashy / **233**. flat / **234**. flat-footed / **235**. flathead / **236**. flat-out / **237**. flattering / **238**. flatulent / **239**. flavored / **240**. flavorless / **241**. flavorsome / **242**. flawed / **243**. flawless / **244**. flaxen / **245**. flea-bitten / **246**. fledged / **247**. fleet / **248**. fleeting / **249**. fleshless / **250**. fleshly / **251**. flesh-shearing / **252**. fleshy / **253**. flexible / **254**. flight-associated / **255**. flightless / **256**. flight-testing / **257**. flighty / **258**. flimsy / **259**. flinty / **260**. flip / **261**. flippant / **262**. flipping / **263**. flirtatious / **264**. floating / **265**. flood-affected / **266**. flood-caused / **267**. flood-dominated / **268**. flood-hit / **269**. flood-like / **270**. flood-prone / **271**. flood-ravaged / **272**. floppy / **273**. floral / **274**. floral-printed / **275**. Florentine / **276**. floury / **277**. flower-bedecked / **278**. flowered / **279**. flowerless / **280**. flowery / **281**. fluent / **282**. fluffy / **283**. fluid / **284**. fluorescent-lit / **285**. flurried / **286**. flush / **287**. flushed / **288**. flustered-sounding / **289**. fluted / **290**. fluvial / **291**. flying / **292**. focal / **293**. fog-enveloped / **294**. foggy / **295**. fog-related / **296**. foldable / **297**. fold-up / **298**. folk / **299**. following / **300**. fond / **301**. food-borne / **302**. food-deprived / **303**. food-filled / **304**. foodless / **305**. food-prone / **306**. foolhardy / **307**. foolish / **308**. foolproof / **309**. football-crazy / **310**. football-related / **311**. football-shaped / **312**. foot-deep / **313**. footless / **314**.

footling / **315**. foot-long / **316**. footloose / **317**. footsore / **318**. forbearing / **319**. forbidden / **320**. forced / **321**. forceful / **322**. forcible / **323**. foregone / **324**. foreign / **325**. foreign-born / **326**. foreigner-friendly / **327**. foreign-made / **328**. foreign-owned / **329**. foremost / **330**. forensic / **331**. foreseeable / **332**. forested / **333**. forfeit / **334**. forgetful / **335**. forgettable / **336**. forgivable / **337**. forgiving / **338**. forked / **339**. forlorn / **340**. formal / **341**. formative / **342**. former / **343**. formidable / **344**. formless / **345**. formulaic / **346**. forthcoming / **347**. forthright / **348**. fortuitous / **349**. forward / **350**. forward-looking / **351**. forward-thinking / **352**. foul / **353**. foul-mouthed / **354**. foul-mouthed / **355**. foundation-laying / **356**. four-dimensional / **357**. four-footed / **358**. four-star / **359**. four-stroke / **360**. foxed / **361**. foxy / **362**. fractious / **363**. fragile / **364**. fragrant / **365**. frail / **366**. Franciscan / **367**. frank / **368**. frantic / **369**. fraternal / **370**. fraudulent / **371**. fraught / **372**. frazzled / **373**. freakish / **374**. freaky / **375**. free / **376**. free on board / **377**. free-floating / **378**. free-flowing / **379**. free-form / **380**. free-hand / **381**. freelance / **382**. free-range / **383**. free-standing / **384**. free-thinking / **385**. free-to-air / **386**. freewheeling / **387**. freezing / **388**. freight-loading / **389**. French / **390**. French-made / **391**. French-owned / **392**. frenzied / **393**. frequent / **394**. frequentative / **395**. frequently expressed / **396**. fresh / **397**. fresh-faced / **398**. freshly constituted / **399**. freshly cooked / **400**. freshly dug / **401**. freshly released / **402**. freshly slaughtered / **403**. freshly trained / **404**. fretful / **405**. fretted / **406**. Freudian / **407**. friable / **408**. frictional / **409**. frictionless / **410**. friendless / **411**. friendly / **412**. frigging / **413**. frightened / **414**. frightening / **415**. frightful / **416**. frigid / **417**. frilled / **418**. frivolous / **419**. frolicsome / **420**. front / **421**. frontal / **422**. front-end / **423**. frosted / **424**. frosty / **425**. frothy / **426**. frugal / **427**. fruit-filled / **428**. fruit-flavored / **429**. fruitful / **430**. fruitless / **431**. fruity / **432**. frustrated / **433**. frustrating / **434**. fuddled / **435**. fuel-consuming / **436**. fuel-filled / **437**. fuel-free / **438**. fuel-guzzling / **439**. fuel-laden / **440**. fugitive / **441**. fulfilled / **442**. fulfilling / **443**. full / **444**. full-blooded / **445**. full-blown / **446**. full-blown / **447**. full-board / **448**. full-bodied / **449**. full-body / **450**. full-color / **451**. full-cream / **452**. full-face / **453**. full-fat / **454**. full-figured / **455**. full-fledged / **456**. full-fledged / **457**. full-frontal / **458**. full-grown / **459**. full-length / **460**. full-page / **461**. full-scale / **462**. full-size / **463**. full-sized / **464**. full-sleeved / **465**. full-term /

466. full-time / 467. fulsome / 468. fumbling / 469. functional / 470. functionalist / 471. functionless / 472. fundamental / 473. funerary / 474. fun-filled / 475. fungal / 476. fungous / 477. funky / 478. fun-loving / 479. funny / 480. furious / 481. furnished / 482. furred / 483. furry / 484. furthest / 485. furtive / 486. fusible / 487. fussy / 488. future / 489. future-oriented / 490. future-proof / 491. fuzzy / 492. fuzzy-cheeked

02g. Useful Adjectives -- 'G'

1. gaga / 2. gag-inducing / 3. gainful / 4. galactic / 5. gallant / 6. galleried / 7. Gallic / 8. galling / 9. galloping / 10. galore / 11. galvanic / 12. game-related / 13. gangling / 14. gangrenous / 15. gap-toothed / 16. garbed / 17. garbled / 18. gargantuan / 19. garish / 20. garrulous / 21. gas-based / 22. gas-cooled / 23. gaseous / 24. gas-fired / 25. gas-permeable / 26. gassy / 27. gastric / 28. gastronomic / 29. gastronomical / 30. gated / 31. gaudy / 32. gaunt / 33. gawky / 34. gay / 35. geared / 36. gelatinous / 37. geminate / 38. genderless / 39. gender-specific / 40. general / 41. generalized / 42. general-purpose / 43. generational / 44. generative / 45. generic / 46. generous / 47. genetic / 48. genetically modified / 49. genital / 50. genteel / 51. gentle / 52. gentlemanly / 53. genuine / 54. geocentric / 55. geo-fencing / 56. geographical / 57. geological / 58. geometric / 59. geometrical / 60. Georgian / 61. geothermal / 62. geriatric / 63. German / 64. German-born / 65. Germanic / 66. germ-covered / 67. getable / 68. ghastly / 69. ghostly / 70. ghoulish / 71. giant / 72. gibbous / 73. giddy / 74. gifted / 75. gift-giving / 76. gigantic / 77. giggly / 78. gilded / 79. gilt-edged / 80. gimcrack / 81. ginger / 82. gingery / 83. girlie / 84. girlish / 85. giveaway / 86. given / 87. glacial / 88. glacier-fed / 89. glad / 90. gladiatorial / 91. gladiolus / 92. glamorous / 93. glamour-filled / 94. glancing / 95. glaring / 96. glassless / 97. glass-walled / 98. glassy / 99. glaucoma-induced / 100. glazed / 101. gleaming / 102. gleeful / 103. glib / 104. glitch-free / 105. glittering / 106. glittery / 107. global / 108. globally wanted / 109. globetrotting / 110. globular / 111. gloomy / 112. glorified / 113. glorious / 114. glossy / 115. gloved / 116. glowing / 117. glum / 118. glutinous / 119. gluttonous / 120. gnarled / 121. gnawing / 122. go-ahead / 123. goalless / 124. god-awful / 125. godforsaken / 126. god-given / 127. godless / 128. godlike / 129. godly / 130. goggle-eyed / 131. go-go / 132. gold / 133. golden / 134. golden-cheeked / 135. gold-plated / 136. golfing / 137. good / 138. good-hearted / 139. goodish / 140. goodly / 141. good-natured / 142. good-tempered / 143. good-time / 144. gooey / 145. goofy / 146. goon-dominated / 147. gorgeous / 148. gory / 149. gothic / 150. governing / 151. government-aided / 152. governmental / 153. government-approved / 154. government-conducted / 155. government-

controlled / **156**. government-funded / **157**. government-held / **158**. government-installed / **159**. government-opposition / **160**. government-owned / **161**. government-run / **162**. gowned / **163**. graceful / **164**. graceless / **165**. gracious / **166**. gradable / **167**. graded / **168**. gradual / **169**. graduated / **170**. graft-ridden / **171**. grained / **172**. grammatical / **173**. grand / **174**. grandiloquent / **175**. grandiose / **176**. granola / **177**. granted / **178**. granular / **179**. graphic / **180**. graphical / **181**. graspable / **182**. grasping / **183**. grassland-dependent / **184**. grassy / **185**. grateful / **186**. gratifying / **187**. grating / **188**. gratuitous / **189**. grave / **190**. gravelly / **191**. grave-looking / **192**. gravid / **193**. gravitational / **194**. gray-cheeked / **195**. grayish / **196**. grayscale / **197**. greasy / **198**. great / **199**. Grecian / **200**. greed-based / **201**. greedy / **202**. green / **203**. green-cheeked / **204**. green-eyed / **205**. greenish / **206**. gregarious / **207**. grief-stricken / **208**. grey-bearded / **209**. grey-haired / **210**. grief-stricken / **211**. grievous / **212**. grievously injured / **213**. grim / **214**. grim-faced / **215**. grinding / **216**. griping / **217**. grisly / **218**. gritty / **219**. grizzled / **220**. groggy / **221**. groomed / **222**. grooved / **223**. groovy / **224**. gross / **225**. grossly polluting / **226**. grotesque / **227**. grouchy / **228**. groundless / **229**. ground-to-air / **230**. growing / **231**. grown-up / **232**. growth-inflation / **233**. growth-oriented / **234**. grubby / **235**. grudging / **236**. grueling / **237**. gruff / **238**. grumpy / **239**. guarded / **240**. gubernatorial / **241**. guessable / **242**. guided / **243**. guiding / **244**. guileless / **245**. guiltless / **246**. guilty / **247**. gulf-based / **248**. gullible / **249**. gummy / **250**. gun-running / **251**. gun-toting / **252**. gun-waving / **253**. gushing / **254**. gusty / **255**. gut / **256**. gut-curdling / **257**. gutless / **258**. gutsy / **259**. gutted / **260**. gut-wrenching / **261**. gym-obsessed

02h. <u>Useful Adjectives</u> -- 'H'

1. habitable / 2. habit-forming / 3. habitual / 4. habituated / 5. hacked off / 6. hackneyed / 7. haggard / 8. hairless / 9. hair-raising / 10. hairy / 11. halcyon / 12. half-and-half / 13. half-baked / 14. half-broken / 15. half-built / 16. half-burnt / 17. half-drawn / 18. half-drowned / 19. half-eaten / 20. half-empty / 21. half-hearted / 22. half-hearted / 23. half-hourly / 24. half-lit / 25. half-price / 26. half-renovated / 27. half-sewn / 28. half-smoked / 29. half-sunken / 30. half-timbered / 31. half-undressed / 32. half-yearly / 33. hallowed / 34. hallucinatory / 35. halting / 36. ham-fisted / 37. hammy / 38. handcrafted / 39. hand-distributed / 40. hand-drafted / 41. handed / 42. hand-held / 43. hand-hot / 44. handicapped / 45. handmade / 46. hands-down / 47. hands-free / 48. hands-off / 49. handsome / 50. hand-to-hand / 51. hand-to-mouth / 52. hand-woven / 53. handwritten / 54. haphazard / 55. haphazardly parked / 56. hapless / 57. happening / 58. happiness boosting / 59. happy / 60. happy-go-lucky / 61. harassed / 62. hard / 63. hard up / 64. hard-bitten / 65. hard-boiled / 66. hard-charging / 67. hard-core / 68. hard-drinking / 69. hard-edged / 70. harder-to-get / 71. hard-faced / 72. hard-fought / 73. hard-headed / 74. hard-hearted / 75. hard-hitting / 76. hard-line / 77. hard-nosed / 78. hard-pressed / 79. hardscrabble / 80. hard-to-access / 81. hard-to-reach / 82. hard-to-see / 83. hard-to-wash-off / 84. hard-wearing / 85. hard-wired / 86. hard-won / 87. hard-working / 88. hardy / 89. harmful / 90. harmless / 91. harmonic / 92. harmonious / 93. harrowing / 94. harsh / 95. hassle-filled / 96. hassle-free / 97. hastily conducted / 98. hastily formed / 99. hastily implemented / 100. hastily organized / 101. hasty / 102. hatchet-faced / 103. hate-driven / 104. hate-filled / 105. hate-fuelled / 106. hateful / 107. hatless / 108. haughty / 109. haunted / 110. haunting / 111. hawk-eyed / 112. hawkish / 113. haywire / 114. hazardous / 115. hazard-prone / 116. hazel / 117. haze-prone / 118. hazy / 119. headed / 120. headless / 121. headline-making / 122. head-mounted / 123. head-on / 124. head-quartered / 125. headstrong / 126. head-to-head / 127. heady / 128. health-centric / 129. health-conscious / 130. healthful / 131. health-related / 132. healthy / 133. heaped / 134. hearable / 135. heart-broken / 136. heartfelt / 137. heartless / 138. heart-rending / 139. heart-shaped / 140. heart-shattering / 141.

heart-stopping / **142**. heart-to-heart / **143**. heart-warming / **144**. heart-wrenching / **145**. hearty / **146**. heat-activated / **147**. heat-aggravated / **148**. heated / **149**. heathen / **150**. heatproof / **151**. heat-related / **152**. heat-resistant / **153**. heat-seeking / **154**. heat-sensitive / **155**. heavenly / **156**. heaven-sent / **157**. heavily armed / **158**. heavily bolted / **159**. heavily criticized / **160**. heavily damaged / **161**. heavily fortified / **162**. heavily guarded / **163**. heavily laden / **164**. heavily muscled / **165**. heavily polluted / **166**. heavily polluting / **167**. heavily wounded / **168**. heaving / **169**. heavy / **170**. heavy-duty / **171**. heavy-handed / **172**. Hebraic / **173**. hectic / **174**. hedonistic / **175**. heedful / **176**. heedless / **177**. hefty / **178**. height-enhancing / **179**. heinous / **180**. heirloom / **181**. helical / **182**. helicopter-borne / **183**. heliocentric / **184**. hell-bent / **185**. Hellenic / **186**. Hellenistic / **187**. hellish / **188**. helmeted / **189**. helmet-less / **190**. helpful / **191**. helpless / **192**. helter-skelter / **193**. hemispherical / **194**. hemorrhagic / **195**. henna-decorated / **196**. henpecked / **197**. hepatic / **198**. herbaceous / **199**. herbal / **200**. herbivorous / **201**. herculean / **202**. hereditary / **203**. heretical / **204**. heritable / **205**. hermeneutic / **206**. hermetic / **207**. hermetical / **208**. heroic / **209**. hesitant / **210**. heterogeneous / **211**. heterozygous / **212**. heuristic / **213**. hexadecimal / **214**. hexagonal / **215**. hidebound / **216**. hideous / **217**. hierarchical / **218**. hieratical / **219**. hieroglyphic / **220**. high / **221**. high-altitude / **222**. high-attended / **223**. high-born / **224**. highbrow / **225**. high-capacity / **226**. high-class / **227**. high-decibel / **228**. high-definition / **229**. high-density / **230**. high-dimensional / **231**. high-elevation / **232**. high-end / **233**. highfalutin / **234**. high-flown / **235**. high-flying / **236**. high-grade / **237**. high-handed / **238**. high-heeled / **239**. high-impact / **240**. high-intensity / **241**. highland / **242**. high-level / **243**. highly acclaimed / **244**. highly ambitious / **245**. highly classified / **246**. highly competitive / **247**. highly decomposed / **248**. highly deflated / **249**. highly educated / **250**. highly enthusiastic / **251**. highly flammable / **252**. highly fortified / **253**. highly individualistic / **254**. highly paid / **255**. highly partisan / **256**. highly placed / **257**. highly polluted / **258**. highly provocative / **259**. highly refuted / **260**. highly regarded / **261**. highly skilled / **262**. highly spiritual / **263**. highly toxic / **264**. highly truncated / **265**. highly vitiated / **266**. high-magnitude / **267**. high-maintenance / **268**. high-minded / **269**. high-octane / **270**. high-performance / **271**. high-pitch /

272. high-pitched / **273**. high-powered / **274**. high-pressure / **275**. high-priced / **276**. high-profile / **277**. high-profile / **278**. high-quality / **279**. high-ranking / **280**. high-returns / **281**. high-rise / **282**. high-risk / **283**. high-security / **284**. high-sounding / **285**. high-speed / **286**. high-spirited / **287**. high-tech / **288**. high-tension / **289**. high-value / **290**. highway-widening / **291**. hilarious / **292**. hind / **293**. hindmost / **294**. hip / **295**. Hispanic / **296**. historic / **297**. historical / **298**. history-making / **299**. histrionic / **300**. hit-and-miss / **301**. hit-and-run / **302**. hittable / **303**. hoarse / **304**. hoary / **305**. hoity-toity / **306**. hole-and-corner / **307**. holistic / **308**. hollow / **309**. hollow-cheeked / **310**. Hollywood-style / **311**. holographic / **312**. holy / **313**. home / **314**. home-based / **315**. home-built / **316**. home-cooked / **317**. home-educated / **318**. homegrown / **319**. homeless / **320**. homely / **321**. home-produced / **322**. home-related / **323**. homespun / **324**. home-style / **325**. homeward / **326**. homey / **327**. homicidal / **328**. homing / **329**. homogenous / **330**. homologous / **331**. homophobic / **332**. homophonous / **333**. homosexual / **334**. homozygous / **335**. honest / **336**. honey-combed / **337**. honeyed / **338**. honorable / **339**. honorary / **340**. honorific / **341**. hooded / **342**. hooked / **343**. hooped / **344**. hoped-for / **345**. hope-filled / **346**. hopeful / **347**. hopeless / **348**. hopping / **349**. horizontal / **350**. hormone-caused / **351**. horn-rimmed / **352**. horny / **353**. horrendous / **354**. horrible / **355**. horrid / **356**. horrific / **357**. horrifically wounded / **358**. horrifying / **359**. horror-stricken / **360**. horror-struck / **361**. horse-drawn / **362**. horse-driven / **363**. horsey / **364**. horticultural / **365**. hospitable / **366**. hospital-acquired / **367**. hospital-borne / **368**. hostile / **369**. hot / **370**. hot-blooded / **371**. hotly contested / **372**. hotly debated / **373**. hot-tempered / **374**. hourglass / **375**. hour-long / **376**. hourly / **377**. housebound / **378**. house-broken / **379**. house-proud / **380**. house-to-house / **381**. house-trained / **382**. housing-related / **383**. howling / **384**. how-to / **385**. huffy / **386**. huge / **387**. huge-accounted / **388**. hulking / **389**. human / **390**. humane / **391**. human-induced / **392**. humanitarian / **393**. humble / **394**. humdrum / **395**. humid / **396**. hummable / **397**. humorless / **398**. humorous / **399**. humor-focused / **400**. hung / **401**. hunger-stricken / **402**. hunger-striking / **403**. hungry / **404**. hunky-dory / **405**. hunted / **406**. hurried / **407**. hurriedly called / **408**. hurriedly convened / **409**. hurt / **410**. hurtful / **411**. hushed / **412**. hush-hush / **413**. husky / **414**. hydraulic / **415**.

hydro-electric / **416**. hydrogenated / **417**. hydrogen-powered / **418**. hydrographical / **419**. hydrophobic / **420**. hydrostatical / **421**. hydrous / **422**. hygienic / **423**. hyped up / **424**. hyperactive / **425**. hyperbolic / **426**. hyperbolical / **427**. hypersensitive / **428**. hypnotic / **429**. hypoallergenic / **430**. hypochondriac / **431**. hypocritical / **432**. hypothetical / **433**. hysterical

02i. <u>Useful</u> <u>Adjectives</u> -- 'I'

1. ice-bound / 2. iced / 3. iconoclastic / 4. icy / 5. icy-clear / 6. ideal / 7. idealistic / 8. ideational / 9. identical / 10. identical-looking / 11. identically worded / 12. identifiable / 13. identity related / 14. ideographical / 15. ideological / 16. idiomatic / 17. idiomatical / 18. idiosyncratic / 19. idiotic / 20. idle / 21. idolatrous / 22. idyllic / 23. iffy / 24. igneous / 25. ignoble / 26. ignominious / 27. ignorable / 28. ignorant / 29. ill / 30. ill-advised / 31. ill-assorted / 32. ill-concealed / 33. ill-conceived / 34. ill-considered / 35. ill-defined / 36. ill-defined / 37. ill-disposed / 38. illegal / 39. illegal-built / 40. illegally owned / 41. illegible / 42. illegitimate / 43. ill-equipped / 44. ill-fated / 45. ill-founded / 46. ill-gotten / 47. illiberal / 48. illimitable / 49. ill-informed / 50. illiterate / 51. ill-judged / 52. ill-mannered / 53. illness-causing / 54. illness-free / 55. illogical / 56. ill-omened / 57. ill-prepared / 58. ill-regulated / 59. ill-starred / 60. ill-tempered / 61. ill-timed / 62. illuminated / 63. illuminating / 64. ill-used / 65. illusive / 66. illustrative / 67. illustrious / 68. ill-ventilated / 69. imaginable / 70. imaginational / 71. imaginative / 72. imitative / 73. immaculate / 74. immanent / 75. immaterial / 76. immature / 77. immeasurable / 78. immediate / 79. immemorial / 80. immense / 81. immersive / 82. immigration-centric / 83. imminent / 84. immiscible / 85. immobile / 86. immoderate / 87. immoral / 88. immortal / 89. immovable / 90. immune-compromised / 91. immunological / 92. immutable / 93. impacted / 94. impaired / 95. impalpable / 96. impartial / 97. impassable / 98. impassioned / 99. impassive / 100. impatient / 101. impeachable / 102. impeccable / 103. impecunious / 104. impending / 105. impenetrable / 106. impenitent / 107. imperative / 108. imperceptible / 109. imperfect / 110. imperial / 111. imperious / 112. imperishable / 113. impermanent / 114. impermeable / 115. impermissible / 116. impersonal / 117. impertinent / 118. imperturbable / 119. impervious / 120. impetuous / 121. impious / 122. impish / 123. implacable / 124. implausible / 125. implementable / 126. implicational / 127. implicit / 128. impolite / 129. imponderable / 130. importable / 131. important / 132. importunate / 133. imposable / 134. imposing / 135. impossible / 136. impossible-to-please / 137. impossible-to-resist / 138. impotent / 139. impoverished / 140. impracticable / 141. impractical / 142. imprecise / 143. impregnable / 144.

impressed / **145**. impressionable / **146**. impressionistic / **147**. improbable / **148**. impromptu / **149**. impromptu called / **150**. improper / **151**. improvable / **152**. improvident / **153**. imprudent / **154**. impudent / **155**. impulsive / **156**. impure / **157**. inaccessible / **158**. inaccurate / **159**. inactive / **160**. inadequate / **161**. inadmissible / **162**. inadvisable / **163**. inalienable / **164**. inane / **165**. inanimate / **166**. inapplicable / **167**. inappropriate / **168**. inarticulate / **169**. inattentive / **170**. inaudible / **171**. inaugural / **172**. inauspicious / **173**. inauthentic / **174**. inbound / **175**. inbounds / **176**. inbred / **177**. inbuilt / **178**. incalculable / **179**. incandescent / **180**. incapable / **181**. incarnate / **182**. incautious / **183**. incendiary / **184**. incensed / **185**. incessant / **186**. incestuous / **187**. inchoative / **188**. incidental / **189**. incipient / **190**. incisive / **191**. inclement / **192**. inclined / **193**. inclusive / **194**. incoherent / **195**. incombustible / **196**. income-generating / **197**. income-oriented / **198**. incoming / **199**. incommensurable / **200**. incommensurate / **201**. incommunicable / **202**. incommunicado / **203**. incomparable / **204**. incompatible / **205**. incompetent / **206**. incomplete / **207**. incomprehensible / **208**. incompressible / **209**. inconceivable / **210**. inconclusive / **211**. incongruous / **212**. inconsequential / **213**. inconsiderable / **214**. inconsiderate / **215**. inconsistent / **216**. inconsolable / **217**. inconspicuous / **218**. inconstant / **219**. incontestable / **220**. incontrovertible / **221**. inconvenient / **222**. incorporable / **223**. incorporated / **224**. incorporeal / **225**. incorrigible / **226**. incorruptible / **227**. incredible / **228**. incredulous / **229**. incumbent / **230**. incurable / **231**. incurious / **232**. indebted / **233**. indecent / **234**. indecipherable / **235**. indecisive / **236**. indeclinable / **237**. indecorous / **238**. indefatigable / **239**. indefeasible / **240**. indefensible / **241**. indefinable / **242**. indelible / **243**. indelicate / **244**. indented / **245**. independent / **246**. independent-minded / **247**. in-depth / **248**. indescribable / **249**. indestructible / **250**. indeterminable / **251**. India-bound / **252**. India-centric / **253**. Indian / **254**. Indian-born / **255**. indicative / **256**. indictable / **257**. indie / **258**. indifferent / **259**. indigenous / **260**. indigenously built / **261**. indigenously developed / **262**. indigent / **263**. indigestible / **264**. indignant / **265**. indiscernible / **266**. indispensable / **267**. indisposed / **268**. indisputable / **269**. indissoluble / **270**. indistinct / **271**. indistinguishable / **272**. individual / **273**. individualized / **274**. individually / **275**. indivisible /

276. indivisible / 277. indo-European / 278. indolent / 279. indomitable / 280. indubitable / 281. inducible / 282. inductive / 283. indulgent / 284. industrial / 285. industrious / 286. industry-oriented / 287. industry-related / 288. inebriated / 289. inedible / 290. ineffable / 291. ineffective / 292. ineffectual / 293. inefficient / 294. inelegant / 295. ineligible / 296. ineluctable / 297. inequitable / 298. ineradicable / 299. inertial / 300. inescapable / 301. inessential / 302. inestimable / 303. inevitable / 304. inexact / 305. inexcusable / 306. inexhaustible / 307. inexorable / 308. inexpedient / 309. inexpensive / 310. inexperienced / 311. inexpert / 312. inexplicable / 313. inexpressible / 314. inextensible / 315. inextinguishable / 316. inextricable / 317. infallible / 318. infamous / 319. infant / 320. infantile / 321. infatuated / 322. infeasible / 323. infected / 324. infection-free / 325. infectious / 326. infective / 327. infelicitous / 328. inferable / 329. inferential / 330. inferior / 331. infernal / 332. infertile / 333. infinite / 334. infinitesimal / 335. infirm / 336. inflamed / 337. inflammable / 338. inflammable parched / 339. inflammatory / 340. inflatable / 341. inflated / 342. inflationary / 343. inflectional / 344. inflexible / 345. influential / 346. informal / 347. informational / 348. information-packed / 349. informative / 350. informed / 351. infrared / 352. infrastructure-starved / 353. infrequent / 354. infuriating / 355. ingenious / 356. ingenuous / 357. inglorious / 358. ingrained / 359. ingratiating / 360. ingredient-driven / 361. inhabitable / 362. inhabited / 363. inharmonious / 364. inherent / 365. inheritable / 366. inhibited / 367. inhomogeneous / 368. inhospitable / 369. in-house / 370. in-human / 371. inhumane / 372. inimical / 373. inimitable / 374. iniquitous / 375. initial / 376. injudicious / 377. injured / 378. injurious / 379. injury-ridden / 380. ink-stained / 381. inky / 382. inlaid / 383. inland / 384. inmost / 385. innate / 386. innermost / 387. innocent / 388. innocent-looking / 389. innocuous / 390. innovational / 391. innovation-based / 392. innovation-oriented / 393. innovative / 394. innuendo-filled / 395. innumerable / 396. innumerate / 397. inoffensive / 398. inoperable / 399. inoperative / 400. inordinate / 401. inorganic / 402. inquisitive / 403. inquisitorial / 404. insalubrious / 405. insane / 406. insanitary / 407. insatiable / 408. inscrutable / 409. insect-infested / 410. insectivorous / 411. insect-ridden / 412. insecure / 413. insensible / 414. insensitive / 415. inseparable / 416. inside / 417. insidious / 418. insightful / 419.

insignificant / **420**. insincere / **421**. insipid / **422**. insistent / **423**. insolent / **424**. insoluble / **425**. insolvent / **426**. inspectional / **427**. inspirational / **428**. inspired / **429**. inspiring / **430**. installable / **431**. instant / **432**. instantaneous / **433**. instinctive / **434**. instinctual / **435**. institutional / **436**. institutionalized / **437**. instruction / **438**. instructional / **439**. instructive / **440**. instrumental / **441**. insubstantial / **442**. insufferable / **443**. insufficient / **444**. insulated / **445**. insulating / **446**. insulting / **447**. insult-ridden / **448**. insuperable / **449**. insupportable / **450**. insured / **451**. insurgency-hit / **452**. insurgency-ridden / **453**. insurmountable / **454**. intact / **455**. intangible / **456**. integral / **457**. integrated / **458**. intellectual / **459**. intelligence-gathering / **460**. intelligent / **461**. intelligible / **462**. intemperate / **463**. intended / **464**. intense / **465**. intensive / **466**. intensive-care / **467**. intent / **468**. intentional / **469**. interactional / **470**. interactive / **471**. interchangeable / **472**. intercollegiate / **473**. interconnected / **474**. intercontinental / **475**. intercultural / **476**. interdepartmental / **477**. interdependent / **478**. interdisciplinary / **479**. interest-bearing / **480**. interested / **481**. interest-free / **482**. interest-free / **483**. interesting / **484**. intergalactic / **485**. interglacial / **486**. intergovernmental / **487**. interim / **488**. interior / **489**. interlinear / **490**. intermediate / **491**. interminable / **492**. intermittent / **493**. internal / **494**. international / **495**. internationally acclaimed / **496**. internationally recognized / **497**. internecine / **498**. internet-based / **499**. interoperable / **500**. interpersonal / **501**. interplanetary / **502**. interpretable / **503**. interpretative / **504**. interracial / **505**. interrelated / **506**. interrogative / **507**. interrogatory / **508**. interstate / **509**. interstellar / **510**. interstitial / **511**. intervening / **512**. interwar / **513**. intestate / **514**. intimate / **515**. intimidated / **516**. intimidating / **517**. intolerable / **518**. intolerant / **519**. intoxicated / **520**. intoxicating / **521**. intractable / **522**. intramural / **523**. intramuscular / **524**. intransigent / **525**. intransitive / **526**. intrauterine / **527**. intravenous / **528**. intrepid / **529**. intricate / **530**. intrigued / **531**. intriguing / **532**. intrinsic / **533**. introductory / **534**. introspective / **535**. intrusive / **536**. intuitive / **537**. invalid / **538**. invaluable / **539**. invariable / **540**. invariant / **541**. invasive / **542**. invective-ridden / **543**. inventive / **544**. inverse / **545**. invertible / **546**. investable / **547**. investigational / **548**. investigative / **549**. investment-driven / **550**. investment-friendly / **551**. inveterate / **552**. invidious / **553**. invincible / **554**.

inviolable / **555**. inviolate / **556**. invisible / **557**. invitational / **558**. inviting / **559**. involuntary / **560**. involved / **561**. invulnerable / **562**. inward / **563**. in-your-face / **564**. irascible / **565**. irascible / **566**. iridescent / **567**. Irish / **568**. irksome / **569**. iron / **570**. iron-boosting / **571**. iron-fisted / **572**. ironic / **573**. ironical / **574**. iron-like / **575**. irrational / **576**. irreconcilable / **577**. irrecoverable / **578**. irredeemable / **579**. irreducible / **580**. irrefutable / **581**. irregular / **582**. irrelevant / **583**. irreligious / **584**. irremediable / **585**. irreparable / **586**. irreplaceable / **587**. irrepressible / **588**. irreproachable / **589**. irreproducible / **590**. irresistible / **591**. irresolute / **592**. irresolvable / **593**. irresponsible / **594**. irretrievable / **595**. irreverent / **596**. irreversible / **597**. irrevocable / **598**. irrigation-related / **599**. irritable / **600**. irritated / **601**. irritating / **602**. isolated / **603**. isolating / **604**. isometric / **605**. isotonic / **606**. issuable / **607**. issue-based / **608**. issue-oriented / **609**. Italianate / **610**. italic / **611**. itchy / **612**. itinerant

02j. Useful Adjectives -- 'J'

1. jack / 2. jaded / 3. jagged / 4. jammed / 5. jam-packed / 6. Japan-style / 7. jaundiced / 8. jaunty / 9. jaw-dropping / 10. jazzed / 11. jazz-obsessed / 12. jazzy / 13. jealous / 14. jellied / 15. jerky / 16. Jewish / 17. jiggered / 18. jinxed / 19. jobbing / 20. job-creating / 21. job-generating / 22. jobless / 23. job-oriented / 24. jocose / 25. joined-up / 26. joint / 27. jolly / 28. journalistic / 29. jovial / 30. joyful / 31. joyless / 32. joyous / 33. jubilant / 34. judgmental / 35. judicial / 36. judicious / 37. juicy / 38. jumbo / 39. jumped-up / 40. junior / 41. junky / 42. juridical / 43. jurisprudential / 44. juristic / 45. just / 46. just released / 47. just-announced / 48. just-concluded / 49. justifiable / 50. justified / 51. just-published / 52. just-readied / 53. juvenile

02k. <u>Useful Adjectives -- 'K'</u>

1. Kafkaesque / 2. kaput / 3. keen / 4. keen-eyed / 5. keenly awaited / 6. keenly contested / 7. keenly fought / 8. kerosene-powered / 9. key / 10. keyed up / 11. kid-centric / 12. kid-oriented / 13. killing / 14. kind / 15. kind-hearted / 16. kindred / 17. kinematical / 18. kinky / 19. kite-caused / 20. kite-flying / 21. kittenish / 22. knee-deep / 23. knee-high / 24. knee-length / 25. knife-toting / 26. knife-wielding / 27. knightly / 28. knitted / 29. knockabout / 30. knock-down / 31. knock-kneed / 32. knock-on / 33. knock-out / 34. knotty / 35. knowable / 36. knowing / 37. knowledgeable / 38. knowledge-based

021. Useful Adjectives -- 'L'

1. lab grown / 2. laboratory-confirmed / 3. labor-driven / 4. labored / 5. labor-intensive / 6. laborious / 7. lackadaisical / 8. lacking / 9. lackluster / 10. laconic / 11. ladylike / 12. laid-back / 13. lame / 14. lamentable / 15. lamented / 16. laminated / 17. land-based / 18. landless / 19. landlocked / 20. landmine-strewn / 21. landslide-hit / 22. landslide-prone / 23. languid / 24. languorous / 25. lanky / 26. lapidary / 27. large / 28. large-hearted / 29. largely peaceful / 30. large-scale / 31. largest-circulated / 32. largish / 33. lascivious / 34. laser-waving / 35. last-ditch / 36. last-ditch / 37. last-gasp / 38. last-minute / 39. last-moment / 40. late / 41. late-night / 42. late-winter / 43. Latin / 44. Latinate / 45. latter / 46. laudable / 47. laughable / 48. laughing / 49. laugh-out-loud / 50. lavish / 51. law-abiding / 52. lawful / 53. lawless / 54. lawyer-dominated / 55. lawyer-turned / 56. lax / 57. lay / 58. lazy / 59. leaded / 60. leaden / 61. leaderless / 62. lead-free / 63. leading / 64. lead-ridden / 65. lead-tainted / 66. leafless / 67. leafy / 68. leaky / 69. learnable / 70. learned / 71. leasehold / 72. leathery / 73. lecherous / 74. leeward / 75. left / 76. left-field / 77. left-footed / 78. left-hand / 79. leftist / 80. leftist-dominated / 81. leftmost / 82. leftward / 83. left-wing / 84. legacy / 85. legal / 86. legalistic / 87. legally compliant / 88. leggy / 89. legible / 90. legion / 91. legislative / 92. legit / 93. legitimate / 94. legless / 95. leguminous / 96. leisured / 97. lemony / 98. lengthy / 99. lenient / 100. leprosy-afflicted / 101. leprosy-stricken / 102. leprous / 103. lethal / 104. lethargic / 105. level-headed / 106. level-playing / 107. lexical / 108. liable / 109. libelous / 110. liberal / 111. liberal-dominated / 112. liberated / 113. Liberian-flagged / 114. libidinous / 115. lice-infested / 116. licentious / 117. lidded / 118. lidless / 119. life-altering / 120. life-changing / 121. life-enhancing / 122. life-giving / 123. lifeless / 124. lifelike / 125. lifelong / 126. life-or-death / 127. life-saving / 128. life-size / 129. life-sized / 130. life-threatening / 131. light / 132. light-colored / 133. lighted / 134. light-emitting / 135. light-fingered / 136. light-footed / 137. light-headed / 138. light-hearted / 139. lightless / 140. lightning / 141. light-skinned / 142. lightweight / 143. like / 144. likeable / 145. likely / 146. like-minded / 147. lily-strewn / 148. lily-white / 149. limbless / 150. limited / 151. limiting / 152. limitless / 153. limp / 154. limpid / 155. lineal / 156. linear / 157. line-

caught / **158**. lined / **159**. lingering / **160**. lingual / **161**. linguistic / **162**. linkable / **163**. lion-hearted / **164**. lippy / **165**. lip-smacking / **166**. liquid / **167**. liquid-filled / **168**. listenable / **169**. listless / **170**. literal / **171**. literary / **172**. literate / **173**. lithographical / **174**. litigious / **175**. litter-filled / **176**. little / **177**. livable / **178**. live / **179**. lived-in / **180**. live-in / **181**. live-long / **182**. lively / **183**. livid / **184**. living / **185**. loadable / **186**. load-bearing / **187**. loaded / **188**. loath / **189**. loathsome / **190**. local / **191**. localized / **192**. locally grown / **193**. locally owned / **194**. locally registered / **195**. locatable / **196**. located / **197**. location-based / **198**. lockable / **199**. locomotive / **200**. lofty / **201**. logarithmical / **202**. logical / **203**. logistical / **204**. London-bound / **205**. lonely / **206**. lonesome / **207**. long / **208**. long-awaited / **209**. long-beaked / **210**. long-believed / **211**. long-billed / **212**. long-cherished / **213**. long-delayed / **214**. long-distance / **215**. long-drawn / **216**. long-drawn-out / **217**. longed-for / **218**. long-established / **219**. long-festering / **220**. long-flowing / **221**. long-haired / **222**. long-haul / **223**. long-held / **224**. longing / **225**. longish / **226**. longitudinal / **227**. long-known / **228**. long-lapsed / **229**. long-last / **230**. long-lasting / **231**. long-life / **232**. long-lived / **233**. long-lost / **234**. long-pending / **235**. long-range / **236**. long-ranging / **237**. long-repressed / **238**. long-running / **239**. long-serving / **240**. long-shuttered / **241**. long-sighted / **242**. long-simmering / **243**. long-sought / **244**. long-standing / **245**. long-standing / **246**. long-stay / **247**. long-suffering / **248**. long-suppressed / **249**. long-term / **250**. long-time / **251**. long-winded / **252**. looks-obsessed / **253**. loony / **254**. loopy / **255**. loose / **256**. loose-leaf / **257**. lopsided / **258**. loquacious / **259**. lordly / **260**. losable / **261**. lost / **262**. lotus-like / **263**. loud / **264**. loud-mouthed / **265**. lousy / **266**. lovable / **267**. loved-up / **268**. loveless / **269**. lovely / **270**. lovesick / **271**. love-struck / **272**. loving / **273**. low / **274**. low hanging / **275**. low-born / **276**. lowbrow / **277**. low-calorie / **278**. low-class / **279**. low-cost / **280**. low-cut / **281**. low-down / **282**. low-end / **283**. low-fat / **284**. low-flying / **285**. low-grade / **286**. low-growing / **287**. low-impact / **288**. low-income / **289**. low-intensity / **290**. low-key / **291**. lowland / **292**. low-level / **293**. lowly / **294**. low-lying / **295**. low-occupancy / **296**. low-paid / **297**. low-paying / **298**. low-pitched / **299**. low-profile / **300**. low-quality / **301**. low-ranking / **302**. low-rent / **303**. low-resolution / **304**. low-rise / **305**. low-risk / **306**. low-rung / **307**. low-tech / **308**. loyal / **309**. loyalist-held / **310**. lubricious / **311**.

lucid / **312**. luckless / **313**. lucky / **314**. lucrative / **315**. ludicrous / **316**. luggage-packed / **317**. lugubrious / **318**. lukewarm / **319**. lumbar / **320**. lumbering / **321**. luminous / **322**. lumpish / **323**. lunatic / **324**. lurid / **325**. luscious / **326**. lush / **327**. lusterless / **328**. lustful / **329**. lustrous / **330**. luxuriant / **331**. luxurious / **332**. lyric / **333**. lyrical

02m. <u>Useful Adjectives</u> -- 'M'

1. macabre / **2**. macho / **3**. macrobiotic / **4**. mad / **5**. madcap / **6**. made-up / **7**. magenta / **8**. maggot-infested / **9**. maggot-ridden / **10**. magic / **11**. magical / **12**. magisterial / **13**. magnanimous / **14**. magnetic / **15**. magnificent / **16**. main / **17**. mainline / **18**. mainstream / **19**. maintainable / **20**. majestic / **21**. major / **22**. maladroit / **23**. male / **24**. male-dominated / **25**. malevolent / **26**. malformed / **27**. malicious / **28**. malign / **29**. malignant / **30**. malleable / **31**. malnutrition-ridden / **32**. malodorous / **33**. malted / **34**. malware-ridden / **35**. mammoth / **36**. manageable / **37**. managed / **38**. managerial / **39**. mandated / **40**. maneuverable / **41**. mange-infested / **42**. mango-flavored / **43**. mangy / **44**. maniac / **45**. manic / **46**. manicured / **47**. manifold / **48**. manipulative / **49**. manly / **50**. manmade / **51**. mannered / **52**. mannish / **53**. manorial / **54**. man-sized / **55**. manual / **56**. marauding / **57**. marbled / **58**. marginal / **59**. marigold-bedecked / **60**. marine / **61**. marital / **62**. maritime / **63**. marked / **64**. marketable / **65**. market-driven / **66**. market-linked / **67**. market-oriented / **68**. maroon / **69**. marquee / **70**. marriageable / **71**. married / **72**. marshmallow-flavored / **73**. marshy / **74**. Martian / **75**. martyred / **76**. marvelous / **77**. masculine / **78**. mass / **79**. massive / **80**. mass-selling / **81**. master / **82**. masterful / **83**. masterly / **84**. matching / **85**. matchless / **86**. material / **87**. materialistic / **88**. maternal / **89**. matriarchal / **90**. matrilineal / **91**. matrimonial / **92**. matronly / **93**. matted / **94**. mature / **95**. maudlin / **96**. mawkish / **97**. maximal / **98**. maximum / **99**. mealy-mouthed / **100**. mean / **101**. meaningful / **102**. meaningless / **103**. means-tested / **104**. measly / **105**. measurable / **106**. measured / **107**. measureless / **108**. meatless / **109**. meaty / **110**. mechanical / **111**. mechanistic / **112**. meddlesome / **113**. medial / **114**. median / **115**. medical / **116**. medically induced / **117**. medical-related / **118**. medicinal / **119**. medico-legal / **120**. medieval / **121**. mediocre / **122**. meditational / **123**. meditative / **124**. medium / **125**. medium-sized / **126**. meek / **127**. meet-and-greet / **128**. megalomaniac / **129**. melancholic / **130**. melancholy / **131**. mellifluous / **132**. mellow / **133**. melodic / **134**. melodious / **135**. melodramatic / **136**. melting / **137**. memorable / **138**. memorial / **139**. menacing / **140**. mendacious / **141**. mendicant / **142**. menial / **143**. menstrual / **144**. mental / **145**. mentally retarded / **146**.

mentholated / **147**. mentionable / **148**. mercenary / **149**. merchant / **150**. merchantable / **151**. merciful / **152**. merciless / **153**. mercurial / **154**. meretricious / **155**. merit-based / **156**. meritorious / **157**. merrily / **158**. merry / **159**. mesmeric / **160**. Mesozoic / **161**. messianic / **162**. messy / **163**. metallic / **164**. metamorphic / **165**. metaphorical / **166**. metaphysical / **167**. meteorological / **168**. methodical / **169**. Methodist / **170**. methodological / **171**. meticulous / **172**. metonymical / **173**. metric / **174**. metrical / **175**. Mexican / **176**. microbial / **177**. microbiological / **178**. microphone-wielding / **179**. microscopic / **180**. microwaveable / **181**. middle / **182**. middle-aged / **183**. middle-class / **184**. middle-distance / **185**. middle-European / **186**. middle-of-the-road / **187**. middle-ranking / **188**. middle-ranking / **189**. midget / **190**. midmost / **191**. mid-range / **192**. mid-sized / **193**. miffed / **194**. mighty / **195**. migratory / **196**. mild / **197**. mildewed / **198**. mild-mannered / **199**. militancy-infested / **200**. militancy-ravaged / **201**. militant / **202**. military / **203**. military-like / **204**. military-style / **205**. milk-producing / **206**. mimetic / **207**. mincing / **208**. mind-bending / **209**. mind-boggling / **210**. mind-boosting / **211**. mindful / **212**. mindless / **213**. mind-numbing / **214**. mind-sapping / **215**. mind-shattering / **216**. mine-protected / **217**. mineral-rich / **218**. miniature / **219**. minimal / **220**. minimalist / **221**. minimum / **222**. miniscule / **223**. ministerial / **224**. ministering / **225**. minister-level / **226**. minor / **227**. minorities-dominated / **228**. minority-owned / **229**. minted / **230**. minty / **231**. minus / **232**. minute / **233**. minute-long / **234**. miraculous / **235**. mired / **236**. mirrored / **237**. mirthless / **238**. misaligned / **239**. misanthropic / **240**. miscellaneous / **241**. mischievous / **242**. miscible / **243**. misconceived / **244**. miserable / **245**. miserly / **246**. misguided / **247**. mishap-prone / **248**. misleading / **249**. misogynistic / **250**. misplaced / **251**. missile-equipped / **252**. missing / **253**. mission-centric / **254**. mistaken / **255**. mistake-ridden / **256**. mistrustful / **257**. misty-eyed / **258**. misunderstood / **259**. mitigating / **260**. mitochondrial / **261**. mixable / **262**. mixed race / **263**. mixed up / **264**. mixed-ability / **265**. mobile-centric / **266**. mobile-friendly / **267**. mocking / **268**. moderate / **269**. moderate-sized / **270**. modern / **271**. modern-day / **272**. modest / **273**. modifiable / **274**. modish / **275**. modular / **276**. moist / **277**. moisture-laden / **278**. moldable / **279**. moldy / **280**. molten / **281**. momentary / **282**. momentous / **283**. monarchial / **284**. monarchical / **285**.

monastic / **286**. monetary / **287**. moneyed / **288**. money-grubbing / **289**. money-hungry / **290**. money-laundering / **291**. moneyless / **292**. money-pooling / **293**. money-saving / **294**. money-spinning / **295**. monkey-infested / **296**. monkish / **297**. monochromatic / **298**. monogamous / **299**. monolingual / **300**. monophonic / **301**. monopolistic / **302**. monosyllabic / **303**. monotone / **304**. monotonous / **305**. monsoon-fed / **306**. monsoon-ravaged / **307**. monster / **308**. monstrous / **309**. month-long / **310**. monthly / **311**. monumental / **312**. mood-altering / **313**. moody / **314**. moon-faced / **315**. moonless / **316**. moonlit / **317**. moon-sized / **318**. moonstruck / **319**. moot / **320**. moral / **321**. moralistic / **322**. morbid / **323**. mordant / **324**. moribund / **325**. morose / **326**. morphological / **327**. mortal / **328**. mosquito-borne / **329**. mosquito-transmitted / **330**. most-valued / **331**. moth-eaten / **332**. motionless / **333**. motivated / **334**. motive / **335**. motiveless / **336**. motley / **337**. motor / **338**. motorcycle-borne / **339**. motorcycle-riding / **340**. motoring / **341**. motorized / **342**. mottled / **343**. mountable / **344**. mountainous / **345**. mounted / **346**. mounting / **347**. mouth-watering / **348**. mouth-watering / **349**. mouthy / **350**. mouthy / **351**. movable / **352**. moving / **353**. much-anticipated / **354**. much-awaited / **355**. much-cited / **356**. much-debated / **357**. much-delayed / **358**. much-desired / **359**. much-discussed / **360**. much-expected / **361**. much-needed / **362**. much-promised / **363**. much-publicized / **364**. much-watched / **365**. muck-dumping / **366**. muddled / **367**. muddle-headed / **368**. muddy / **369**. mud-smeared / **370**. mud-soaked / **371**. muffled / **372**. muggy / **373**. mulled / **374**. multi-agency / **375**. multi-brand / **376**. multi-channel / **377**. multi-colored / **378**. multi-cornered / **379**. multicultural / **380**. multidimensional / **381**. multi-dimensional / **382**. multidisciplinary / **383**. multi-eyed / **384**. multifaceted / **385**. multifarious / **386**. multi-front / **387**. multifunctional / **388**. multigrain / **389**. multi-institutional / **390**. multilateral / **391**. multi-layered / **392**. multilevel / **393**. multilingual / **394**. multi-location / **395**. multimedia / **396**. multimillion / **397**. multi-mouthed / **398**. multinational / **399**. multinuclear / **400**. multi-organ / **401**. multi-phased / **402**. multiple / **403**. multiple-access / **404**. multipronged / **405**. multipurpose / **406**. multiracial / **407**. multi-skill / **408**. multispecialty / **409**. multitudinous / **410**. multi-user / **411**. multi-utility / **412**. Mumbai-bound / **413**. mundane / **414**. municipal / **415**. munificent / **416**. murderous / **417**. murky / **418**. muscle-bound / **419**. muscular / **420**. mushy / **421**. musical / **422**. music-centric / **423**. musk-scented / **424**. Muslim-dominated / **425**. mustached / **426**. musty / **427**. mutable / **428**. mutant / **429**. mutational / **430**. muted / **431**. mutinous / **432**. mutual / **433**. muzzy / **434**. myopic / **435**. myriad / **436**. mysterious / **437**. mystical / **438**. mythic / **439**. mythical

02n. Useful Adjectives -- 'N'

1. nagging / 2. nail-biting / 3. naked / 4. namby-pamby / 5. nameless / 6. narcotic / 7. narrow / 8. narrow-minded / 9. narrow-mouthed / 10. nasal / 11. nascent / 12. nastiest-looking / 13. natal / 14. national / 15. nationalistic / 16. nationally televised / 17. native / 18. natty / 19. natural / 20. natural-born / 21. naturalistic / 22. naturally formed / 23. naughty / 24. nauseous / 25. nautical / 26. naval / 27. navigable / 28. navy blue / 29. near / 30. nearby / 31. near-freezing / 32. nearsighted / 33. neat / 34. neatly folded / 35. nebulous / 36. necessary / 37. neck-deep / 38. need-based / 39. needful / 40. needless / 41. needy / 42. negative / 43. neglected / 44. neglectful / 45. negligent / 46. negligible / 47. negotiable / 48. neighboring / 49. neighborly / 50. neoclassical / 51. neoconservative / 52. Neolithic / 53. neonatal / 54. nerveless / 55. nerve-wrecking / 56. nervous / 57. nervy / 58. net / 59. nethermost / 60. nettlesome / 61. network-centric / 62. neural / 63. neurological / 64. neurotic / 65. neuter / 66. neutral / 67. never-before-used / 68. never-ending / 69. never-in-demand / 70. never-seen-before / 71. new / 72. newborn / 73. newly appointed / 74. newly carved / 75. newly constructed / 76. newly created / 77. newly elected / 78. newly formed / 79. newly inaugurated / 80. newly installed / 81. newly launched / 82. newly married / 83. newly opened / 84. newly set / 85. newlywed / 86. newspaper-wrapped / 87. newsy / 88. next / 89. next-door / 90. nice-looking / 91. nickel-and-dime / 92. nifty / 93. niggardly / 94. night-long / 95. nimble / 96. nitrogenous / 97. nitrous / 98. noble / 99. nocturnal / 100. no-good / 101. noise-induced / 102. noiseless / 103. noisy / 104. nominal / 105. nominative / 106. non-adversarial / 107. non-alcoholic / 108. non-aligned / 109. non-alphabetic / 110. non-biodegradable / 111. nonchalant / 112. non-committal / 113. non-compliance / 114. non-conforming / 115. non-contributory / 116. non-controversial / 117. non-cooperation / 118. non-custodial / 119. nondescript / 120. non-distant / 121. non-domesticated / 122. non-essential / 123. non-executive / 124. non-existent / 125. non-fictional / 126. non-finite / 127. non-flammable / 128. non-flexible / 129. non-fulfillment / 130. non-gradable / 131. non-human / 132. non-invasive / 133. non-linear / 134. non-malignant / 135. non-native / 136. non-negotiable /

137. non-partisan / **138**. non-planned / **139**. nonplussed / **140**. non-potable / **141**. non-prescription / **142**. non-professional / **143**. non-proprietary / **144**. non-refundable / **145**. non-renewable / **146**. non-resident / **147**. non-residential / **148**. non-restrictive / **149**. non-returnable / **150**. non-scientific / **151**. nonsensical / **152**. non-serious / **153**. non-slip / **154**. non-smoking / **155**. non-specific / **156**. non-standard / **157**. non-stick / **158**. non-stop / **159**. non-traditional / **160**. non-union / **161**. non-verbal / **162**. non-vintage / **163**. non-violent / **164**. noonday / **165**. normal / **166**. normal-sized / **167**. normative / **168**. north / **169**. north-bound / **170**. north-easterly / **171**. north-eastern / **172**. northerly / **173**. northern / **174**. northernmost / **175**. north-westerly / **176**. north-western / **177**. nostalgic / **178**. notable / **179**. noted / **180**. noticeable / **181**. notional / **182**. notorious / **183**. novel / **184**. novelty / **185**. now-defunct / **186**. now-junked / **187**. now-shut / **188**. noxious / **189**. nubile / **190**. nuclear / **191**. nuclear-armed / **192**. nuclear-free / **193**. nuclear-tipped / **194**. nude / **195**. nudie / **196**. nugatory / **197**. numb / **198**. numbered / **199**. numberless / **200**. numbing / **201**. numerical / **202**. numerous / **203**. numinous / **204**. nuptial / **205**. nut-brown / **206**. nut-covered / **207**. nutritious / **208**. nymphomaniac

<u>02o.</u> <u>Useful</u> <u>Adjectives</u> -- '<u>O</u>'

1. oaken / **2**. obedient / **3**. obese / **4**. obesity-related / **5**. objectionable / **6**. objective / **7**. objectless / **8**. obligated / **9**. obligatory / **10**. obliged / **11**. obliging / **12**. oblique / **13**. oblivious / **14**. obnoxious / **15**. obscene / **16**. obscure / **17**. obsequious / **18**. observable / **19**. observant / **20**. observational / **21**. obsessive / **22**. obsolete / **23**. obstetrical / **24**. obstinate / **25**. obstreperous / **26**. obstructive / **27**. obtainable / **28**. obtrusive / **29**. obtuse / **30**. obvious / **31**. occasional / **32**. occult / **33**. occupational / **34**. occupied / **35**. oceanfront / **36**. ocean-going / **37**. ocular / **38**. odd / **39**. odds-on / **40**. odious / **41**. odoriferous / **42**. odorless / **43**. odorous / **44**. off-air / **45**. off-duty / **46**. offending / **47**. offensive / **48**. offhand / **49**. official / **50**. officious / **51**. off-limits / **52**. off-peak / **53**. off-piste / **54**. off-putting / **55**. off-road / **56**. off-screen / **57**. offset / **58**. offshore / **59**. offside / **60**. offstage / **61**. off-white / **62**. oft-neglected / **63**. oft-quoted / **64**. oft-quoted / **65**. oft-repeated / **66**. oil-bearing / **67**. oil-fired / **68**. oil-free / **69**. oil-mixed / **70**. oil-rich / **71**. oil-soaked / **72**. oily / **73**. old / **74**. old-fashioned / **75**. old-style / **76**. old-time / **77**. old-world / **78**. oleaginous / **79**. olfactory / **80**. olive / **81**. Olympian / **82**. ominous / **83**. omissible / **84**. omnibus / **85**. omnipotent / **86**. omnipresent / **87**. omniscient / **88**. omnivorous / **89**. on-air / **90**. on-board / **91**. once-bustling / **92**. once-unthinkable / **93**. once-vibrant / **94**. oncoming / **95**. on-demand / **96**. one-dimensional / **97**. one-eyed / **98**. one-man / **99**. one-off / **100**. one-on-one / **101**. onerous / **102**. one-sided / **103**. one-star / **104**. one-stop / **105**. one-time / **106**. one-woman / **107**. ongoing / **108**. only / **109**. on-off / **110**. on-screen / **111**. on-shore / **112**. onstage / **113**. on-street / **114**. onward / **115**. opaque / **116**. open / **117**. open-air / **118**. open-door / **119**. open-ended / **120**. open-handed / **121**. opening / **122**. open-jaw / **123**. open-line / **124**. open-minded / **125**. open-mouthed / **126**. open-necked / **127**. open-pit / **128**. open-plan / **129**. open-source / **130**. operable / **131**. operational / **132**. operationally versatile / **133**. operative / **134**. ophthalmic / **135**. opinionative / **136**. opportune / **137**. opportunistic / **138**. opposed / **139**. opposing / **140**. opposite / **141**. oppositional / **142**. opposition-backed / **143**. opposition-ruled / **144**. opposition-sponsored / **145**. oppressed / **146**. oppressive / **147**. opprobrious / **148**. optical / **149**. optimal / **150**. optimistic

/ **151**. optional / **152**. opulent / **153**. oracular / **154**. oral / **155**. orange-filled / **156**. oratorical / **157**. orbital / **158**. ordered / **159**. orderly / **160**. ordinary / **161**. organic / **162**. organically formed / **163**. organized / **164**. orgiastic / **165**. oriental / **166**. original / **167**. ornamental / **168**. ornate / **169**. ornithological / **170**. orthodox / **171**. orthographical / **172**. Orwellian / **173**. ostensible / **174**. ostentatious / **175**. other-worldly / **176**. out-and-out / **177**. outboard / **178**. outbound / **179**. outdated / **180**. outdoor / **181**. outer / **182**. outermost / **183**. outgoing / **184**. outlandish / **185**. outlying / **186**. outmost / **187**. out-of-date / **188**. out-of-pocket / **189**. out-of-state / **190**. out-of-the-way / **191**. out-of-town / **192**. out-of-work / **193**. outrage-evoking / **194**. outrageous / **195**. outright / **196**. outside / **197**. outspoken / **198**. outspread / **199**. outstanding / **200**. outstretched / **201**. out-there / **202**. outward / **203**. outward-looking / **204**. outworn / **205**. oval / **206**. oven proof / **207**. oven-ready / **208**. over easy / **209**. overactive / **210**. overage / **211**. overall / **212**. overambitious / **213**. overanxious / **214**. overarching / **215**. overbearing / **216**. overblown / **217**. overcast / **218**. overcautious / **219**. overconfident / **220**. overcrowded / **221**. overdeveloped / **222**. overdrawn / **223**. overdressed / **224**. overdue / **225**. overexcited / **226**. overextended / **227**. overgenerous / **228**. overgrown / **229**. overhead / **230**. overheated / **231**. overinflated / **232**. overjoyed / **233**. overlong / **234**. overmanned / **235**. overnight / **236**. over-occupied / **237**. over-optimistic / **238**. overpopulated / **239**. overpowering / **240**. overpriced / **241**. over-priced / **242**. overprotective / **243**. overriding / **244**. overripe / **245**. overseas / **246**. oversensitive / **247**. oversized / **248**. over-sized / **249**. overstaffed / **250**. over-strained / **251**. oversubscribed / **252**. overt / **253**. over-the-counter / **254**. overtired / **255**. overweening / **256**. overweight / **257**. overwhelming / **258**. overworked / **259**. overwrought / **260**. oviparous / **261**. ovoviviparous / **262**. owing / **263**. owlish / **264**. own / **265**. owner-occupied / **266**. oxygen-depleted / **267**. oxygen-starved / **268**. ozone-depleting

02p. Useful Adjectives -- 'P'

1. pacific / 2. packable / 3. paddy-growing / 4. paid / 5. paid-up / 6. pained / 7. painful / 8. painless / 9. painstaking / 10. painterly / 11. paint-smeared / 12. palatable / 13. palatial / 14. palatine / 15. pale / 16. pale-cheeked / 17. paleographical / 18. Paleozoic / 19. palliative / 20. pallid / 21. palpable / 22. paltry / 23. Panamanian flagged / 24. panama-registered / 25. pandemic / 26. panegyric / 27. panic-driven / 28. panicky / 29. panic-stricken / 30. panoramic / 31. pantheistical / 32. paperless / 33. paper-made / 34. paper-thin / 35. parabolic / 36. paradigmatic / 37. paralinguistic / 38. parallel / 39. paralytic / 40. paramedic / 41. paramedical / 42. parametrical / 43. paramilitary / 44. paranoid / 45. paranormal / 46. paraplegic / 47. parasitic / 48. parasitical / 49. parched / 50. pardonable / 51. parental / 52. parenthetical / 53. parish-pump / 54. parliamentary / 55. parlous / 56. parochial / 57. parsimonious / 58. partial / 59. partially damaged / 60. participatory / 61. particular / 62. particulate / 63. partisan / 64. part-time / 65. part-way / 66. party-loving / 67. passable / 68. passenger-centric / 69. passing / 70. passionate / 71. passionless / 72. passive / 73. past / 74. pastoral / 75. pasty / 76. pat / 77. patchable / 78. patchy / 79. patent / 80. patentable / 81. paternal / 82. path-breaking / 83. pathetic / 84. pathetical / 85. pathless / 86. pathological / 87. patient / 88. patient-centric / 89. patriarchal / 90. patrician / 91. patriotic / 92. patterned / 93. paunchy / 94. payable / 95. pay-for-performance / 96. peaceable / 97. peaceful / 98. peacekeeping / 99. peace-loving / 100. peach / 101. pea-green / 102. peak / 103. pear-shaped / 104. pebbly / 105. pectoral / 106. peculiar / 107. pecuniary / 108. pedagogic / 109. pedagogical / 110. pedantic / 111. pedestrian / 112. pedestrian-friendly / 113. pedigree / 114. peerless / 115. peeved / 116. peevish / 117. pejorative / 118. pelagic / 119. pellucid / 120. penal / 121. pen-and-ink / 122. pending / 123. pendulous / 124. penetrable / 125. penetrating / 126. penetrative / 127. peninsular / 128. penitent / 129. penniless / 130. penny-pinching / 131. pensionable / 132. pensive / 133. pentagonal / 134. pentatonic / 135. pent-up / 136. penultimate / 137. penurious / 138. people-centric / 139. people-oriented / 140. peppery / 141. peppy / 142. perceivable / 143. percent / 144. perceptible / 145. perceptional / 146. perception-driven /

147. perceptive / 148. perceptual / 149. perched / 150. percipient / 151. percussive / 152. peremptory / 153. perennial / 154. perfect / 155. perfidious / 156. performable / 157. performance-based / 158. performance-centric / 159. performance-enhancing / / 160. perfunctory / 161. perilous / 162. period / 163. periodic / 164. periodical / 165. peripatetic / 166. peripheral / 167. perishable / 168. perished / 169. perishing / 170. permanent / 171. permeable / 172. permissible / 173. permissive / 174. pernicious / 175. perpendicular / 176. perpetual / 177. perplexed / 178. persevering / 179. persistent / 180. personable / 181. personal / 182. person-to-person / 183. perspicacious / 184. perspicuous / 185. perspiration-soaked / 186. persuasive / 187. pertinacious / 188. pertinent / 189. pervasive / 190. perverse / 191. perverted / 192. pesky / 193. pessimistic / 194. pesticide-spraying / 195. pesticide-tainted / 196. pestilential / 197. pet / 198. petite / 199. petrified / 200. petrol- or diesel-fired / 201. petroleum-based / 202. petrol-filled / 203. petrol-powered / 204. petrol-soaked / 205. pettish / 206. petty / 207. phallic / 208. phantom / 209. pharmaceutical / 210. pharyngeal / 211. phenomenal / 212. philharmonic / 213. philosophical / 214. phlegmatic / 215. phone-equipped / 216. phonetic / 217. phony / 218. phosphorescent / 219. photoelectric / 220. photoelectrical / 221. photogenic / 222. photographic / 223. photographical / 224. photometrical / 225. photosensitive / 226. physical / 227. picaresque / 228. pick-and-mix / 229. pickled / 230. pickup / 231. picky / 232. pictorial / 233. picture-perfect / 234. picturesque / 235. piddling / 236. piecemeal / 237. pie-eyed / 238. piercing / 239. piffling / 240. pigeon-toed / 241. piggy / 242. pig-headed / 243. pig-ignorant / 244. pigmented / 245. pillared / 246. pilot / 247. pinched / 248. pink / 249. pink-cheeked / 250. pink-collar / 251. pink-colored / 252. pinkish / 253. pinpoint accuracy / 254. pint-sized / 255. pioneering / 256. pious / 257. piping / 258. piquant / 259. pirate-infested / 260. pitch-black / 261. pitch-dark / 262. pitched / 263. piteous / 264. pithy / 265. pitiable / 266. pitiful / 267. pitiless / 268. pitted / 269. pitying / 270. pivotal / 271. placard-wielding / 272. placatory / 273. placental / 274. placid / 275. plain / 276. plain-clothed / 277. plaintive / 278. plane / 279. planetary / 280. plangent / 281. plantar / 282. plant-based / 283. plant-filled / 284. plastered / 285. plastic / 286. plastic-related / 287. plate-sized / 288. platitudinous / 289. platonic /

290. plausible / 291. playable / 292. played out / 293. playful / 294. pleasant / 295. pleased / 296. pleasing / 297. pleasurable / 298. plebeian / 299. plenary / 300. plenteous / 301. plentiful / 302. pliable / 303. pliant / 304. plodding / 305. plug-in / 306. plum / 307. plumed / 308. plump / 309. plump-cheeked / 310. plumy / 311. plunging / 312. plural / 313. pluralist / 314. plus / 315. plush / 316. plus-sized / 317. pneumatic / 318. pocked / 319. pocket-sized / 320. podgy / 321. poetic / 322. poetical / 323. po-faced / 324. poignant / 325. point-and-click / 326. point-and-shoot / 327. point-blank / 328. pointed / 329. pointless / 330. pointy / 331. poised / 332. poisonous / 333. poker-faced / 334. poky / 335. polar / 336. polemical / 337. police-involved / 338. policy-centric / 339. policy-oriented / 340. polio-stricken / 341. polish / 342. polished / 343. polite / 344. politic / 345. political / 346. politically crucial / 347. politically driven / 348. politically incorrect / 349. politically influential / 350. politically motivated / 351. politically motivated / 352. politically tumultuous / 353. politically unstable / 354. politically vital / 355. politically volatile / 356. politician-led / 357. poll-related / 358. pollution-checking / 359. pollution-free / 360. pollution-measuring / 361. pollution-related / 362. polyandrous / 363. polygamous / 364. polyglot / 365. polyhedral / 366. polymorphous / 367. polyvalent / 368. pompous / 369. ponderous / 370. pond-like / 371. pontifical / 372. pooped / 373. poor / 374. pop / 375. pop-eyed / 376. popish / 377. popular / 378. popularly held / 379. population-specific / 380. populist / 381. populous / 382. porcine / 383. porky / 384. porous / 385. portable / 386. portentous / 387. portly / 388. portmanteau / 389. portrait / 390. Portuguese / 391. posh / 392. positional / 393. positive / 394. possessed / 395. possessive / 396. possible / 397. postal / 398. post-delivery / 399. posterior / 400. poster-making / 401. post-free / 402. post-harvest / 403. post-haste / 404. posthumous / 405. post-industrial / 406. postmodern / 407. post-operation / 408. post-paid / 409. post-partition / 410. postprandial / 411. post-retirement / 412. post-study / 413. postural / 414. potable / 415. pot-bellied / 416. potent / 417. potential / 418. pothole-free / 419. pothole-infested / 420. pothole-ridden / 421. potted / 422. pourable / 423. poverty-centric / 424. poverty-stricken / 425. powder blue / 426. powdered / 427. powdery / 428. power-deficient / 429. powerful / 430. powerless / 431. power-obsessed / 432. power-related / 433. power-

sharing / **434**. power-starved / **435**. power-tripping / **436**. practicable / **437**. practical / **438**. practiced / **439**. pragmatic / **440**. preachy / **441**. prearranged / **442**. precancerous / **443**. precarious / **444**. precariously tilted / **445**. precautionary / **446**. precious / **447**. precipitate / **448**. precipitous / **449**. precise / **450**. precision-guided / **451**. precocious / **452**. preconscious / **453**. precooked / **454**. predatory / **455**. pre-dawn / **456**. predestined / **457**. predicative / **458**. predictable / **459**. predictive / **460**. predigested / **461**. predominant / **462**. pre-eminent / **463**. pre-emptive / **464**. preferable / **465**. preferential / **466**. pre-filled / **467**. pregnancy-induced / **468**. pregnant / **469**. prehistoric / **470**. prejudiced / **471**. prejudicial / **472**. preliminary / **473**. premature / **474**. premeditated / **475**. premier / **476**. premised / **477**. premium / **478**. premium-quality / **479**. prenatal / **480**. preoccupied / **481**. preoperational / **482**. preordained / **483**. pre-owned / **484**. pre-packed / **485**. prepaid / **486**. preparatory / **487**. prepared / **488**. preponderant / **489**. prepossessing / **490**. preposterous / **491**. pre-prandial / **492**. pre-production / **493**. pre-qualifying / **494**. pre-requisite / **495**. prescient / **496**. prescriptive / **497**. present / **498**. presentable / **499**. presentational / **500**. presidential / **501**. presidential-type / **502**. pressed / **503**. pressing / **504**. pre-stamped / **505**. prestige / **506**. prestigious / **507**. presumable / **508**. presumptive / **509**. presumptuous / **510**. pre-tax / **511**. pretend / **512**. pretentious / **513**. preternatural / **514**. pretty / **515**. prevailing / **516**. prevalent / **517**. preventable / **518**. preventative / **519**. preventive / **520**. preverbal / **521**. previous / **522**. pre-war / **523**. price-controlled / **524**. priceless / **525**. pricey / **526**. prickly / **527**. prim / **528**. prima facie / **529**. primal / **530**. primary / **531**. prime / **532**. primitive / **533**. primordial / **534**. princely / **535**. principal / **536**. principled / **537**. printable / **538**. prior / **539**. prismatic / **540**. prissy / **541**. pristine / **542**. privacy-centric / **543**. private / **544**. private-funded / **545**. privately funded / **546**. privately owned / **547**. privileged / **548**. prize / **549**. prized / **550**. prize-giving / **551**. pro rata / **552**. proactive / **553**. probabilistic / **554**. probable / **555**. probing / **556**. problematic / **557**. problematical / **558**. problem-focused / **559**. problem-oriented / **560**. problem-plagued / **561**. processional / **562**. procrustean / **563**. procurable / **564**. pro-democracy / **565**. prodigal / **566**. prodigious / **567**. producible / **568**. productive / **569**. profane / **570**. profanity-laced / **571**. pro-feminist /

572. professed / 573. professional / 574. professionally trained / 575. professorial / 576. proficient / 577. profitable / 578. profitless / 579. profit-making / 580. profligate / 581. profound / 582. profuse / 583. programmable / 584. programmatic / 585. progressive / 586. prohibitive / 587. project-based / 588. pro-liberal / 589. prolific / 590. prolix / 591. prolonged / 592. prominent / 593. promiscuous / 594. promotable / 595. promotional / 596. prompt / 597. prone / 598. pronominal / 599. pronounceable / 600. pronounced / 601. proof / 602. proper / 603. propertied / 604. property-related / 605. prophetic / 606. prophylactic / 607. propitiatory / 608. propitious / 609. proportional / 610. proportioned / 611. propositional / 612. proprietary / 613. prosaic / 614. prosecutable / 615. prospective / 616. prosperous / 617. prostrate / 618. protean / 619. protective / 620. protracted / 621. proud / 622. provable / 623. proverbial / 624. provident / 625. providential / 626. provincial / 627. provisional / 628. provocative / 629. proximal / 630. proximate / 631. prudent / 632. prudential / 633. prudish / 634. prurient / 635. pseudonymous / 636. psychiatric / 637. psychic / 638. psychical / 639. psychoanalytical / 640. psychological / 641. psychometric / 642. psychometrical / 643. psychosomatic / 644. psychotropic / 645. pubic / 646. public / 647. publicity-seeking / 648. publicly-listed / 649. public-minded / 650. public-related / 651. publishable / 652. puckish / 653. puerile / 654. puffed / 655. puffy / 656. puffy-cheeked / 657. pugilistic / 658. pugnacious / 659. pull-down / 660. pull-out / 661. pulp / 662. pump-action / 663. punchy / 664. punctilious / 665. punctual / 666. pungent / 667. punishable / 668. punishing / 669. punitive / 670. puny / 671. purchasable / 672. pure / 673. purebred / 674. puritanical / 675. purple / 676. purplish / 677. purported / 678. purpose-built / 679. purposeful / 680. purposeless / 681. purposive / 682. pursuant / 683. purulent / 684. pushed / 685. pushy / 686. putative / 687. putrid / 688. put-upon / 689. puzzled / 690. pygmy / 691. pyramid-shaped / 692. pyrotechnical

<u>02q.</u> <u>Useful</u> <u>Adjectives</u> -- '<u>Q</u>'

1. quadrangular / 2. quadraphonic / 3. quadriplegic / 4. quaint / 5. quake-affected / 6. quake-battered / 7. quake-hit / 8. qualified / 9. qualitative / 10. quality / 11. quantifiable / 12. quantitative / 13. quarrelsome / 14. quasi-autonomous / 15. quasi-civilian / 16. quasi-failed / 17. quasi-judicial / 18. quasi-public / 19. quasi-sovereign / 20. queasy / 21. queenly / 22. queer / 23. querulous / 24. questionable / 25. questioning / 26. quick / 27. quick-fire / 28. quicksilver / 29. quick-tempered / 30. quick-witted / 31. quiescent / 32. quiet / 33. quilted / 34. quintessential / 35. quintuple / 36. quixotic / 37. quizzical / 38. quotable / 39. quotidian

<u>02r.</u> <u>Useful</u> <u>Adjectives</u> -- 'R'

1. rabbinical / 2. rabid / 3. racial / 4. racially charged / 5. racially motivated / 6. racy / 7. radar-evading / 8. radial / 9. radiant / 10. radiation-infested / 11. radiation-laced / 12. radical / 13. radical-sounding / 14. radish / 15. rage-filled / 16. ragged / 17. raging / 18. ragtag / 19. rain-affected / 20. rain-bearing / 21. rainbow-beaked / 22. rainbow-colored / 23. rainbow-hued / 24. rain-fed / 25. rain-free / 26. rain-hit / 27. rain-induced / 28. rain-infested / 29. rainless / 30. rain-marred / 31. rain-ravaged / 32. rain-slicked / 33. rain-soaked / 34. rain-spawned / 35. rain-sufficient / 36. rain-swollen / 37. rain-swollen / 38. rain-triggered / 39. rainy / 40. raked / 41. rakish / 42. rambling / 43. rampant / 44. ramshackle / 45. rancorous / 46. random / 47. rank / 48. ranking / 49. rapacious / 50. rapid / 51. rapid-fire / 52. rapidly increasing / 53. rapidly-deployable / 54. rapt / 55. rapturous / 56. rare / 57. rarefied / 58. raring / 59. rash / 60. rashly driven / 61. raspy / 62. ratable / 63. rat-infested / 64. rational / 65. ratty / 66. raucous / 67. raunchy / 68. raven / 69. ravening / 70. ravenous / 71. raving / 72. ravishing / 73. razor-beaked / 74. razor-thin / 75. reachable / 76. reactive / 77. reactivity / 78. readable / 79. ready / 80. ready-made / 81. ready-mixed / 82. ready-to-eat / 83. ready-to-harvest / 84. ready-to-wear / 85. real / 86. realistic / 87. realizable / 88. real-life / 89. real-world / 90. rear / 91. rearmost / 92. rearward / 93. reasonable / 94. reasonably priced / 95. reasoned / 96. reasonless / 97. reassuring / 98. rebel-held / 99. rebel-infested / 100. rebellious / 101. reborn / 102. rebuttable / 103. recalcitrant / 104. receivable / 105. received / 106. recent / 107. recently concluded / 108. recently elected / 109. recently employed / 110. recently held / 111. recently inaugurated / 112. recently reconstituted / 113. recently released / 114. recently released / 115. recently resumed / 116. recently rich / 117. receptive / 118. recession-hit / 119. recessive / 120. rechargeable / 121. reciprocal / 122. reckless / 123. reckonable / 124. reclaimable / 125. recognizable / 126. recommendable / 127. reconcilable / 128. recondite / 129. reconfigurable / 130. reconstructive / 131. recordable / 132. record-loving / 133. recoverable / 134. recreant / 135. recreational / 136. rectifiable / 137. rectilinear / 138. recumbent / 139. recuperative / 140. recurrent / 141. recursive / 142. recyclable / 143. red / 144. red-beaconed

/ 145. reddish / 146. redeemable / 147. redemptive / 148. red-faced / 149. red-hot / 150. redistributable / 151. redistributive / 152. redolent / 153. redoubtable / 154. reducible / 155. reductive / 156. redundant / 157. referable / 158. referential / 159. refillable / 160. refined / 161. reflective / 162. reflexive / 163. reform-centric / 164. reformist / 165. reformist-backed / 166. reform-minded / 167. refractive / 168. refractory / 169. refreshable / 170. refreshing / 171. refulgent / 172. refundable / 173. refutable / 174. regal / 175. regardless / 176. regency / 177. regimental / 178. regimented / 179. regional / 180. regional-level / 181. regressive / 182. regretful / 183. regrettable / 184. regular / 185. regulatory / 186. related / 187. relational / 188. relative / 189. relaxed / 190. relaxing / 191. releasable / 192. relentless / 193. relevant / 194. reliable / 195. reliant / 196. relief seekers / 197. relieved / 198. religion-based / 199. religious / 200. reluctant / 201. remaining / 202. remarkable / 203. remediable / 204. remedial / 205. reminiscent / 206. remiss / 207. remorseless / 208. remote / 209. remote-controlled / 210. removable / 211. remunerative / 212. renal-related / 213. renewable / 214. renewed / 215. renowned / 216. rent-free / 217. repairable / 218. repayable / 219. repeatable / 220. repeated / 221. repeatedly-used / 222. repellent / 223. repentant / 224. repetitious / 225. repetitive / 226. replaceable / 227. replete / 228. replicable / 229. reportable / 230. reprehensible / 231. representational / 232. representative / 233. repressed / 234. repressive / 235. reproachful / 236. rep-roaring / 237. reproducible / 238. reproductive / 239. republican / 240. republican-dominated / 241. repulsive / 242. reputable / 243. reputational / 244. reputed / 245. requisite / 246. research-oriented / 247. resentful / 248. reserved / 249. resettable / 250. resident / 251. residential / 252. residual / 253. residuary / 254. resigned / 255. resilient / 256. resistant / 257. resistible / 258. resistive / 259. resolute / 260. resolvable / 261. resonant / 262. resounding / 263. resourceful / 264. resource-rich / 265. resource-saving / 266. respectable / 267. respectful / 268. respective / 269. respiratory / 270. resplendent / 271. responsible / 272. responsive / 273. rested / 274. restful / 275. restive / 276. restless / 277. restorative / 278. restrained / 279. restricted / 280. restrictive / 281. resultant / 282. result-oriented / 283. resurgent / 284. retaining / 285. retarded / 286. reticent / 287. reticulated / 288. retired / 289. retractable / 290. retrievable

/ **291**. retrograde / **292**. retrogressive / **293**. retrospective / **294**. returnable / **295**. reusable / **296**. revealing / **297**. revelatory / **298**. reverent / **299**. reverential / **300**. reversible / **301**. reviewable / **302**. revisable / **303**. revisionist / **304**. revivalist / **305**. revocable / **306**. revolt-hit / **307**. revolting / **308**. revolutionary / **309**. revolving / **310**. rewarding / **311**. rewritable / **312**. rhetorical / **313**. rhythmical / **314**. ribald / **315**. ribbed / **316**. ribbon-cutting / **317**. rice-shelling / **318**. rich / **319**. rickety / **320**. ride-sharing / **321**. ridged / **322**. ridiculous / **323**. rife / **324**. right / **325**. right-angled / **326**. righteous / **327**. rightful / **328**. right-hand / **329**. right-handed / **330**. rightist / **331**. right-minded / **332**. rightmost / **333**. rightward / **334**. rigid / **335**. rigorous / **336**. rimless / **337**. ringing / **338**. ring-shaped / **339**. rinky-dink / **340**. riot-hit / **341**. riotous / **342**. riot-ravaged / **343**. risible / **344**. risk-averse / **345**. risk-based / **346**. risk-prone / **347**. risky / **348**. ritual / **349**. ritualistic / **350**. rival / **351**. roast / **352**. roasting / **353**. robot-assisted / **354**. robotic / **355**. robust / **356**. rock solid / **357**. rocket-propelled / **358**. rock-hard / **359**. rodent-infested / **360**. rogue / **361**. roguish / **362**. rollicking / **363**. roll-on / **364**. roly-poly / **365**. roman / **366**. romantic / **367**. roofless / **368**. roof-ripping / **369**. roomy / **370**. rootless / **371**. rope-like / **372**. rose-colored / **373**. rose-scented / **374**. rose-waving / **375**. rosy-cheeked / **376**. rotary / **377**. rotatable / **378**. rotational / **379**. rotten / **380**. rotund / **381**. rough / **382**. rough-and-ready / **383**. round / **384**. roundabout / **385**. round-cheeked / **386**. rounded / **387**. round-eyed / **388**. round-table / **389**. round-the-clock / **390**. rousing / **391**. routine / **392**. roving / **393**. rowdy / **394**. royal / **395**. rubbery / **396**. rubbish-filled / **397**. rubbishy / **398**. rubicund / **399**. rudderless / **400**. ruddy / **401**. rude / **402**. rudimentary / **403**. rueful / **404**. ruffled / **405**. rugged / **406**. ruined / **407**. ruinous / **408**. ruled / **409**. ruling / **410**. ruminative / **411**. runaway / **412**. run-down / **413**. running / **414**. runny / **415**. rural / **416**. rural-centric / **417**. rushed / **418**. russet / **419**. Russian / **420**. Russian-drafted / **421**. Russian-speaking / **422**. rust-colored / **423**. rustic / **424**. rust-laden / **425**. ruthless

02s. Useful Adjectives -- 'S'

1. sacerdotal / 2. sacramental / 3. sacred / 4. sacrificial / 5. sacrilegious / 6. sacrosanct / 7. sad / 8. safe / 9. sagacious / 10. sage-like / 11. saggy / 12. saintly / 13. salable / 14. salacious / 15. saleable / 16. saline / 17. sallow / 18. salted / 19. salt-flavored / 20. salubrious / 21. salvageable / 22. same / 23. sanctimonious / 24. sanctions-hit / 25. sand-laden / 26. sandy / 27. sanguine / 28. sanitary / 29. sapient / 30. sardonic / 31. sartorial / 32. sassy / 33. sated / 34. satin / 35. satirical / 36. satisfactory / 37. satisfied / 38. satisfying / 39. saturated / 40. saucy / 41. savage / 42. savannah-like / 43. savory / 44. scabrous / 45. scalable / 46. scalar / 47. scalding / 48. scam-hit / 49. scam-ridden / 50. scam-riddled / 51. scam-tainted / 52. scandalous / 53. scandal-plagued / 54. scandal-scarred / 55. scanty / 56. scarce / 57. scared / 58. scarf-clad / 59. scarlet / 60. scathing / 61. scatological / 62. scattered / 63. scented / 64. scentless / 65. schematic / 66. schizoid / 67. schizophrenic / 68. scholastic / 69. school-going / 70. school-oriented / 71. sciatic / 72. scientific / 73. scintillating / 74. scooped / 75. scorching / 76. scoreless / 77. scornful / 78. scot-free / 79. Scottish / 80. scraggly / 81. scraggy / 82. scrappy / 83. scratch / 84. scratchy / 85. scrawny / 86. screwed-up / 87. screwy / 88. scripted / 89. scrollable / 90. scrubby / 91. scruffy / 92. scrummy / 93. scrumptious / 94. scrupulous / 95. sculptured / 96. scurrilous / 97. seaborne / 98. sea-facing / 99. sea-green / 100. seamed / 101. seamless / 102. seamy / 103. searchable / 104. searching / 105. searing / 106. seasick / 107. seasonable / 108. seasonal / 109. seasoned / 110. sebaceous / 111. secluded / 112. secondary / 113. second-biggest / 114. second-fastest / 115. second-oldest / 116. second-rate / 117. second-rung / 118. secret / 119. secretarial / 120. secretive / 121. sectarian / 122. sectional / 123. secular / 124. secular-leaning / 125. secure / 126. security-centric / 127. security-cleared / 128. security-driven / 129. security-related / 130. sedate / 131. sedatives-laced / 132. sedentary / 133. sedimentary / 134. seditious / 135. seductive / 136. sedulous / 137. seeable / 138. seeded / 139. seedless / 140. seedy / 141. seeming / 142. seemingly angry / 143. seemingly effortless / 144. seemingly unstoppable / 145. seemly / 146. seep / 147. segmental / 148. segregationist / 149. seismically active / 150.

seismic-resistant / **151**. seismological / **152**. select / **153**. selectable / **154**. selective / **155**. self-absorbed / **156**. self-addressed / **157**. self-adhesive / **158**. self-appointed / **159**. self-assembly / **160**. self-assertive / **161**. self-assured / **162**. self-catering / **163**. self-centered / **164**. self-confessed / **165**. self-confident / **166**. self-congratulation / **167**. self-conscious / **168**. self-contained / **169**. self-contradictory / **170**. self-control / **171**. self-correcting / **172**. self-criticism / **173**. self-defeating / **174**. self-defensive / **175**. self-deprecating / **176**. self-deprecating / **177**. self-directed / **178**. self-drive / **179**. self-educated / **180**. self-effacing / **181**. self-employed / **182**. self-evident / **183**. self-fulfilling / **184**. self-healing / **185**. selfie-obsessed / **186**. self-important / **187**. self-imposed / **188**. self-induced / **189**. self-induced / **190**. self-indulgent / **191**. self-inflicted / **192**. self-inflicted / **193**. self-interested / **194**. selfish / **195**. selfless / **196**. self-made / **197**. self-motivated / **198**. self-opinionated / **199**. self-perpetuating / **200**. self-possessed / **201**. self-proclaimed / **202**. self-referential / **203**. self-regulating / **204**. self-reliant / **205**. self-respecting / **206**. self-righteous / **207**. self-same / **208**. self-satisfied / **209**. self-seeking / **210**. self-service / **211**. self-serving / **212**. self-styled / **213**. self-sufficient / **214**. self-supporting / **215**. self-sustained / **216**. self-taught / **217**. self-wiled / **218**. semantic / **219**. semi-automatic / **220**. semi-clad / **221**. semiconscious / **222**. semi-darkness / **223**. semi-detached / **224**. seminal / **225**. semi-official / **226**. semi-precious / **227**. semi-prepared / **228**. semi-skilled / **229**. semi-skimmed / **230**. semi-stitched / **231**. Semitic / **232**. senior / **233**. sensational / **234**. sensation-driven / **235**. senseless / **236**. sensible / **237**. sensitive / **238**. sensory / **239**. sensuous / **240**. sententious / **241**. sentient / **242**. separable / **243**. separate / **244**. separated / **245**. septic / **246**. sepulchral / **247**. sequential / **248**. sequestered / **249**. seraphic / **250**. serendipitous / **251**. serial / **252**. serious / **253**. serpentine / **254**. serrated / **255**. serried / **256**. server-based / **257**. serviceable / **258**. service-oriented / **259**. service-oriented / **260**. servile / **261**. settled / **262**. severable / **263**. several / **264**. severe / **265**. sexless / **266**. sexual / **267**. shabby / **268**. shade-bearing / **269**. shadow / **270**. shady / **271**. shaggy / **272**. shakable / **273**. shaky / **274**. shallow / **275**. sham / **276**. shambolic / **277**. shamefaced / **278**. shameful / **279**. shameless / **280**. shaming / **281**. shaped / **282**. shapeless / **283**. shapely / **284**. sharable / **285**. shark-filled / **286**. shark-infested / **287**. sharp / **288**. sharp-eyed / **289**. shattered / **290**. shattering / **291**. shatter-proof / **292**. sheepish / **293**. sheer / **294**. shell-shocked / **295**. sheltered / **296**. shiftless / **297**. shingled / **298**. shingly / **299**. shiny / **300**. shippable / **301**. shirtless / **302**. shock-headed / **303**. shock-induced / **304**. shocking / **305**. shockproof / **306**. shod / **307**. shoddy / **308**. shoeless / **309**. shoestring / **310**. shore-based / **311**. short-beaked / **312**. shorthanded / **313**. short-lived / **314**. short-sighted / **315**. short-staffed / **316**. short-stay / **317**. short-tempered / **318**. short-term / **319**. short-term focused / **320**. shoulder-high / **321**. showery / **322**. showy / **323**. shrewd / **324**. shrill / **325**. shrinkable / **326**. shrunken / **327**. shut / **328**. shuttered / **329**. shy / **330**. sick / **331**. sickening / **332**. sickly / **333**. side-long / **334**. side-splitting / **335**. sighted / **336**. sightless / **337**. signal / **338**. significant / **339**. silencer-fitted / **340**. silent / **341**. silky / **342**. silly / **343**. silver-cheeked / **344**. silver-haired / **345**. silvery / **346**. simian / **347**. similar / **348**. simpatico / **349**. simple / **350**. simple-minded / **351**. simplistic / **352**. simulated / **353**. simulating / **354**. simultaneous / **355**. sincere / **356**. sinewy / **357**. single / **358**. single handed / **359**. single-minded / **360**. single-use / **361**. sing-song / **362**. singular / **363**. sinister / **364**. sink / **365**. sinkable / **366**. sinless / **367**. sinuous / **368**. situated / **369**. situational / **370**. six-decade-long / **371**. sizeable / **372**. sizzling / **373**. skanky / **374**. skeletal / **375**. skeleton-smuggling / **376**. skeptical / **377**. sketchy / **378**. skewed / **379**. skilful / **380**. skilled / **381**. skimpy / **382**. skin-deep / **383**. skin-friendly / **384**. skinless / **385**. skinny / **386**. skittish / **387**. skull-shaped / **388**. sky-blue / **389**. sky-high / **390**. skyscraper-studded / **391**. sky-touching / **392**. slanderous / **393**. slangy / **394**. slanted / **395**. slanting / **396**. slapdash / **397**. slap-happy / **398**. slap-up / **399**. slate-grey / **400**. slatted / **401**. slavish / **402**. sleazy / **403**. sleek / **404**. sleep-deprived / **405**. sleep-inducing / **406**. sleepless / **407**. sleepy / **408**. sleepy-eyed / **409**. sleeveless / **410**. slender / **411**. slick / **412**. slight / **413**. slinky / **414**. slippery / **415**. slipshod / **416**. slithery / **417**. slogan-shouting / **418**. sloppy / **419**. sloshed / **420**. slothful / **421**. slouchy / **422**. slovenly / **423**. slow-flowing / **424**. slow-witted / **425**. sludge-covered / **426**. sluggish / **427**. slumped / **428**. sly / **429**. small / **430**. small-bore / **431**. smallish / **432**. small-minded / **433**. small-scale / **434**. small-time / **435**. smarmy / **436**. smart / **437**. smash-and-grab / **438**. smashed / **439**. smelly / **440**. smitten /

441. smog-blanketed / 442. smog-covered / 443. smog-hit / 444. smog-plagued / 445. smoke-emitting / 446. smoke-filled / 447. smoke-free / 448. smokeless / 449. smoke-spewing / 450. smoky / 451. smooth / 452. smooth-talking / 453. smudge-cheeked / 454. smudgy / 455. smutty / 456. snail-paced / 457. snake-infested / 458. snaky / 459. snap / 460. snappy / 461. snarky / 462. snazzy / 463. sneaking / 464. sneaky / 465. snide / 466. snippy / 467. sniveling / 468. snobbish / 469. snooty / 470. snotty / 471. snotty-nosed / 472. snow-affected / 473. snow-bound / 474. snow-clad / 475. snow-covered / 476. snow-fed / 477. snow-laden / 478. snub-nosed / 479. snug / 480. soaking / 481. soapy / 482. sober / 483. sobering / 484. so-called / 485. sociable / 486. social / 487. socialistic / 488. socially conscious / 489. socially excluded / 490. socially selective / 491. socio-biological / 492. socio-cultural / 493. socio-economic / 494. socio-political / 495. socio-political / 496. sodden / 497. soft / 498. soft-boiled / 499. soft-core / 500. soft-hearted / 501. softly-softly / 502. soft-spoken / 503. soft-spoken / 504. software-enabled / 505. soggy / 506. soignée / 507. solar / 508. solar-oriented / 509. solar-powered / 510. soldierly / 511. sole / 512. solemn / 513. solicitous / 514. solid / 515. solid-state / 516. solitary / 517. solo / 518. soluble / 519. solvable / 520. solvent / 521. somber / 522. sometime / 523. somnolent / 524. sonic / 525. sonorous / 526. sophisticated / 527. soporific / 528. soppy / 529. sordid / 530. sore / 531. sorrowful / 532. sorry / 533. sorted / 534. soul-destroying / 535. soulful / 536. soulless / 537. soul-stirring / 538. sound / 539. soundless / 540. soup-like / 541. soupy / 542. sour / 543. sour-faced / 544. south / 545. southbound / 546. south-east / 547. south-eastern / 548. southern / 549. southernmost / 550. south-south-west / 551. south-west / 552. south-westerly / 553. sovereign / 554. space-based / 555. space-constrained / 556. space-starved / 557. spacious / 558. span / 559. Spanish / 560. spanking / 561. spare / 562. sparing / 563. sparkling / 564. sparse / 565. sparsely populated / 566. Spartan / 567. spasmodic / 568. spastic / 569. spatial / 570. special / 571. specialized / 572. specially designed / 573. specifiable / 574. specific / 575. specious / 576. spectacular / 577. spectral / 578. speculative / 579. speechless / 580. speedy / 581. spellbinding / 582. spent / 583. spider-infested / 584. spidery / 585. spiffy / 586. spiked / 587. spiky / 588. spinal / 589. spindly / 590. spine-chilling / 591. spineless

/ **592**. spine-tingling / **593**. spiny / **594**. spirited / **595**. spiritless / **596**. spiritual / **597**. spiritualized / **598**. spiritually charged / **599**. spiteful / **600**. splashy / **601**. splendid / **602**. splenetic / **603**. splinters-laden / **604**. split-level / **605**. split-second / **606**. splitting / **607**. spoilt / **608**. spoken / **609**. spongy / **610**. spontaneous / **611**. spooky / **612**. sporadic / **613**. sporty / **614**. spotless / **615**. spotted / **616**. spotty / **617**. sprawled / **618**. sprawling / **619**. spread-eagled / **620**. sprightly / **621**. spring-loaded / **622**. spruce / **623**. spunky / **624**. spurious / **625**. squalid / **626**. squally / **627**. square / **628**. squared / **629**. squat / **630**. squeaky / **631**. squeamish / **632**. squidgy / **633**. squirrely / **634**. squishy / **635**. stabbing / **636**. stable / **637**. stacked / **638**. stage-struck / **639**. staggering / **640**. stagnant / **641**. staid / **642**. stained / **643**. stained / **644**. stainless / **645**. stale / **646**. stalwart / **647**. stampede-like / **648**. standard / **649**. stand-by / **650**. standing / **651**. stand-offish / **652**. stand-up / **653**. staple / **654**. star-bedecked / **655**. starchy / **656**. star-crossed / **657**. stark / **658**. starless / **659**. star-lit / **660**. starry-eyed / **661**. star-studded / **662**. startling / **663**. start-up / **664**. startup-centric / **665**. starvation-hit / **666**. state of the art / **667**. state-advised / **668**. state-by-state / **669**. state-dominated / **670**. state-funded / **671**. stateless / **672**. state-level / **673**. stately / **674**. state-owned / **675**. state-run / **676**. state-sponsored / **677**. state-wise / **678**. static / **679**. statistical / **680**. statuesque / **681**. statutory / **682**. staunch / **683**. stay-at-home / **684**. steadfast / **685**. steadily dropping / **686**. steadily rising / **687**. steady / **688**. steady-flowing / **689**. stealth / **690**. stealthy / **691**. steam-driven / **692**. steaming / **693**. steamy / **694**. steel-reinforced / **695**. steerable / **696**. stellar / **697**. stenographical / **698**. stentorian / **699**. stereographical / **700**. stereoscopic / **701**. sterile / **702**. sterling / **703**. stern / **704**. stern-looking / **705**. stewed / **706**. stick-on / **707**. sticky / **708**. stiff / **709**. stiff-necked / **710**. still / **711**. still-born / **712**. still-in-shock / **713**. still-smoldering / **714**. stilted / **715**. stingy / **716**. stinking / **717**. stinky / **718**. stir-crazy / **719**. stirring / **720**. stock / **721**. stocky / **722**. stoical / **723**. stoked / **724**. stolid / **725**. stomach-churning / **726**. stone cold / **727**. stone dead / **728**. stone deaf / **729**. stone-faced / **730**. stone-hearted / **731**. stone-throwing / **732**. stonewashed / **733**. stoniness / **734**. stony / **735**. stooped / **736**. stoppable / **737**. storable / **738**. storied / **739**. storm-dominated / **740**. storming / **741**. storm-ravaged / **742**. storm-related / **743**. storm-tossed / **744**. stormy /

745. stout / 746. straggly / 747. straight / 748. straight forward / 749. straight-faced / 750. straight-haired / 751. straight-talking / 752. straitened / 753. strait-laced / 754. strange / 755. strangulated / 756. strapless / 757. strappy / 758. strategically located / 759. strawberry-flavored / 760. stray / 761. streaky / 762. street / 763. streetwise / 764. strenuous / 765. stress-busting / 766. stressed / 767. stress-free / 768. stressful / 769. stress-induced / 770. stress-related / 771. stress-timed / 772. stretchable / 773. stretchy / 774. stricken / 775. strict / 776. strictly-controlled / 777. strident / 778. strife-hit / 779. strife-torn / 780. strike-bound / 781. strike-crippled / 782. strike-prone / 783. striking / 784. string / 785. stringent / 786. stringy / 787. striped / 788. stripped-down / 789. stripy / 790. strong / 791. strongly worded / 792. strong-minded / 793. strong-willed / 794. stroppy / 795. structural / 796. struggle-ridden / 797. stubble-cheeked / white-cheeked / 798. stubby / 799. stuck / 800. studded / 801. studied / 802. studious / 803. study-related / 804. stuffed / 805. stuffy / 806. stultifying / 807. stumpy / 808. stunning / 809. stunted / 810. stupendous / 811. stupid / 812. sturdy / 813. style-conscious / 814. stylish / 815. stylistic / 816. stylized / 817. styptic / 818. suave / 819. sub-aqua / 820. subatomic / 821. subconscious / 822. subcutaneous / 823. subdued / 824. subject / 825. subjective / 826. sublime / 827. subliminal / 828. submarine / 829. submersible / 830. submissive / 831. subnormal / 832. subordinate / 833. subpar / 834. subprime / 835. subsequent / 836. subsidiary / 837. subsonic / 838. substandard / 839. substantial / 840. substantive / 841. substitutable / 842. subtle / 843. subtropical / 844. suburban / 845. subversive / 846. successful / 847. successive / 848. succinct / 849. succulent / 850. sudden / 851. sufficient / 852. suffocating / 853. sugar-coated / 854. sugar-lowering / 855. sugary / 856. suggestible / 857. suggestive / 858. suicidal / 859. suicide-prevention / 860. suicide-related / 861. suitable / 862. suited / 863. sulky / 864. sullen / 865. sultry / 866. summary / 867. summery / 868. sumptuous / 869. sun-baked / 870. sunburned / 871. sun-drenched / 872. sun-dried / 873. sundry / 874. sunken / 875. sunken-cheeked / 876. sun-kissed / 877. sunless / 878. sunlit / 879. sunny / 880. sunset / 881. sunset-tinged / 882. sun-washed / 883. superannuated / 884. superb / 885. supercharged / 886. supercilious / 887. superficial / 888. superfluous / 889. superhuman / 890. superior /

891. superlative / 892. supernatural / 893. superscript / 894. supersize / 895. super-sized / 896. supersonic / 897. superstitious / 898. supine / 899. supple / 900. supply-driven / 901. supply-side / 902. supportable / 903. supporting / 904. supportive / 905. suppressible / 906. supranational / 907. supreme / 908. sure / 909. sure-footed / 910. surface-to-air / 911. surface-to-surface / 912. surgical / 913. surmountable / 914. surplus / 915. surprised / 916. surprising / 917. surreal / 918. surreptitious / 919. surrounding / 920. survivable / 921. susceptible / 922. suspense-filled / 923. suspicious / 924. suspicious-looking / 925. sustainable / 926. swanky / 927. swappable / 928. Swedish / 929. Swedish-born / 930. sweeping / 931. sweet / 932. sweetish / 933. sweet-smelling / 934. swell / 935. sweltering / 936. swift / 937. swimmable / 938. swish / 939. switchable / 940. switched on / 941. swollen / 942. syllabic / 943. syllogistic / 944. symbiotic / 945. symbolic / 946. symbolical / 947. symmetrical / 948. sympathetic / 949. symptomatic / 950. symptomless / 951. synchronic / 952. synchronous / 953. syncopated / 954. synergistic / 955. synonymous / 956. syntactic / 957. syntactical / 958. synthetic / 959. syrupy / 960. systematic / 961. systematical / 962. system-generated / 963. systemic / 964. systems-driven

02t. <u>Useful Adjectives</u> -- 'T'

1. tablet-based / 2. tabloid / 3. tabloid-driven / 4. taciturn / 5. tacky / 6. tactful / 7. tactical / 8. tactile / 9. tactless / 10. tailless / 11. tailor-made / 12. tainted / 13. taint-free / 14. talentless / 15. talkative / 16. tall / 17. tame / 18. tamper-proof / 19. tamping / 20. tan / 21. tangential / 22. tangible / 23. tangled / 24. tanned / 25. Tanzania-born / 26. tapeless / 27. tardy / 28. target-oriented / 29. tasteful / 30. tasteless / 31. tasty / 32. tattered / 33. tatty / 34. taut / 35. tawdry / 36. taxable / 37. tax-deferred / 38. tax-exempt / 39. tax-free / 40. taxing / 41. taxonomical / 42. taxpayer-friendly / 43. tax-related / 44. teachable / 45. teacher-led / 46. tea-growing / 47. tear-filled / 48. tearful / 49. tearless / 50. tear-off / 51. tear-stained / 52. teary-eyed / 53. technical / 54. technically challenging / 55. technically sound / 56. technological / 57. technologically complex / 58. technology-backed / 59. technology-centric / 60. technology-denied / 61. technology-driven / 62. technology-enabled / 63. tedious / 64. teeming / 65. teenaged / 66. teeny / 67. teeth-whitening / 68. teetotal / 69. telepathic / 70. telescopic / 71. tell-all / 72. telling / 73. telltale / 74. temperamental / 75. temperate / 76. temperature-controlled / 77. tempestuous / 78. temporal / 79. temporary / 80. tempting / 81. tenable / 82. tenacious / 83. tendentious / 84. tender / 85. tenor / 86. tense / 87. tensile / 88. tension-hit / 89. tension-ridden / 90. tentative / 91. tented / 92. tenuous / 93. tenured / 94. tepid / 95. terminal / 96. terminally ill / 97. terraced / 98. terrestrial / 99. terrible / 100. terrified / 101. territorial / 102. terror-afflicted / 103. terror-free / 104. terrorism-related / 105. terrorist-infested / 106. terrorists-dominated / 107. terror-linked / 108. terror-ridden / 109. terror-spreading / 110. terror-stricken / 111. terror-struck / 112. tertiary / 113. testable / 114. testimonial / 115. tetchy / 116. textbook / 117. textural / 118. textured / 119. Thai-owned / 120. thankful / 121. thankless / 122. theatrical / 123. thematic / 124. themed / 125. theoretical / 126. theory-based / 127. therapeutic / 128. thermal / 129. thermonuclear / 130. thick / 131. thickheaded / 132. thickly forested / 133. thickly populated / 134. thick-skinned / 135. thin / 136. thinkable / 137. thinking / 138. thinly populated / 139. thinly veiled / 140. thin-walled / 141. third-degree / 142. third-rate / 143. thirsty / 144. thorny / 145. thoughtful / 146. thoughtless / 147. thought-provoking / 148.

thousand-headed / **149**. threatening / **150**. three-cornered / **151**. three-dimensional / **152**. threefold / **153**. three-piece / **154**. three-quarter / **155**. three-star / **156**. three-way / **157**. thriftless / **158**. thrifty / **159**. thrilled / **160**. thrilling / **161**. thrill-seeking / **162**. throaty / **163**. throne-shaped / **164**. through / **165**. throwaway / **166**. thumb-impressed / **167**. thunderous / **168**. thunderstruck / **169**. ticketed / **170**. ticket-issuing / **171**. ticklish / **172**. tidal / **173**. tidy / **174**. tieless / **175**. tiger-bearing / **176**. tiger-centric / **177**. tight / **178**. tight-fisted / **179**. tight-fitting / **180**. tight-lipped / **181**. tiles-making / **182**. time-bound / **183**. time-consuming / **184**. time-lapse / **185**. timeless / **186**. timely / **187**. time-poor / **188**. time-release / **189**. time-saving / **190**. time-tested / **191**. time-worn / **192**. timid / **193**. timorous / **194**. tinny / **195**. tin-roofed / **196**. tiny / **197**. tipsy / **198**. tip-top / **199**. tip-up / **200**. tired / **201**. tired-looking / **202**. tireless / **203**. tiring / **204**. titanic / **205**. titled / **206**. tobacco-related / **207**. toeless / **208**. together / **209**. token / **210**. tolerable / **211**. tolerant / **212**. toll-free / **213**. tonal / **214**. tone-deaf / **215**. toneless / **216**. tongue-in-cheek / **217**. tongue-tied / **218**. tony / **219**. tooled / **220**. toothed / **221**. toothless / **222**. toothsome / **223**. toothy / **224**. top / **225**. top secret / **226**. top-class / **227**. top-down / **228**. top-end / **229**. top-grossing / **230**. top-heavy / **231**. top-hole / **232**. topical / **233**. top-level / **234**. topmost / **235**. top-notch / **236**. topographical / **237**. top-ranking / **238**. top-rated / **239**. top-selling / **240**. top-shelf / **241**. topsy-turvy / **242**. torrential / **243**. torrential / **244**. torrid / **245**. tortuous / **246**. tortured / **247**. torturous / **248**. total / **249**. touch-and-go / **250**. touched / **251**. touching / **252**. touchy / **253**. touchy-feely / **254**. tough / **255**. tough-looking / **256**. tough-minded / **257**. tourism-based / **258**. tourist-carrying / **259**. tourist-driven / **260**. tourist-friendly / **261**. tournament-oriented / **262**. towering / **263**. toxic / **264**. toxicological / **265**. toy / **266**. traceable / **267**. traceless / **268**. trackless / **269**. tractable / **270**. tradable / **271**. traditional / **272**. traditionalist / **273**. traffic-infested / **274**. tragic / **275**. traitorous / **276**. tranquilizer-toting / **277**. transatlantic / **278**. transcendent / **279**. transcendental / **280**. transcontinental / **281**. transferable / **282**. transformational / **283**. transgender / **284**. transgenic / **285**. transient / **286**. transitive / **287**. transit-oriented / **288**. transitory / **289**. translatable / **290**. translucent / **291**. transmissible / **292**. transmittable / **293**. transnational / **294**. transparent / **295**. transportable / **296**. transposable /

297. trappable / **298**. trash-covered / **299**. trashy / **300**. traumatic / **301**. travelling / **302**. travel-related / **303**. travel-sick / **304**. treacherous / **305**. treasonable / **306**. treasonous / **307**. treatable / **308**. treatment-related / **309**. treble / **310**. tree-based / **311**. tree-cutting / **312**. tree-filled / **313**. treeless / **314**. tree-planting / **315**. tremendous / **316**. tremulous / **317**. trendy / **318**. triangular / **319**. tribal / **320**. tribal-dominated / **321**. tri-band / **322**. trick / **323**. tricky / **324**. tried / **325**. triennial / **326**. trifling / **327**. trigger-happy / **328**. trilateral / **329**. trilingual / **330**. trim / **331**. triple / **332**. trite / **333**. triumphal / **334**. triumphant / **335**. trivial / **336**. trochaic / **337**. Trojan / **338**. trophy / **339**. tropical / **340**. troubled / **341**. trouble-free / **342**. trouble-prone / **343**. troublesome / **344**. trouble-torn / **345**. true / **346**. true-blue / **347**. true-life / **348**. trusty / **349**. truthful / **350**. try-and-buy / **351**. trying / **352**. tsunami-crippled / **353**. tsunami-induced / **354**. tsunami-struck / **355**. tubby / **356**. tubeless / **357**. tubular / **358**. tufted / **359**. tumbledown / **360**. tumultuous / **361**. tunable / **362**. tuned in / **363**. tuneful / **364**. tuneless / **365**. turbulent / **366**. turgid / **367**. Turkish / **368**. turmoil-ridden / **369**. tutorial / **370**. tweedy / **371**. twilight / **372**. twilit / **373**. twin / **374**. twin-edged / **375**. twisted / **376**. twist-filled / **377**. twisty / **378**. twitchy / **379**. two-dimensional / **380**. two-edged / **381**. two-faced / **382**. two-fold / **383**. two-footed / **384**. two-handed / **385**. two-ply / **386**. two-stroke / **387**. two-way / **388**. typewritten / **389**. type-written / **390**. typical / **391**. typo-ridden / **392**. tyrannical / **393**. tyrannous

02u. Useful Adjectives -- 'U'

1. U.S.-born / 2. U.S.-operated / 3. U.S.-owned / 4. UK-built / 5. ulcerous / 6. ultimate / 7. ultra-accurate / 8. ultra-bright / 9. ultra-cheap / 10. ultra-cold / 11. ultra-conservative / 12. ultra-efficient / 13. ultra-fast / 14. ultra-high / 15. ultra-intelligent / 16. ultra-light / 17. ultra-likeable / 18. ultra-long / 19. ultra-loose / 20. ultra-low / 21. ultra-luxurious / 22. ultra-nationalist / 23. ultra-orthodox / 24. ultra-plush / 25. ultra-precision / 26. ultra-private / 27. ultra-processed / 28. ultra-productive / 29. ultra-rich / 30. ultra-rugged / 31. ultra-secure / 32. ultra-sensitive / 33. ultra-slow / 34. ultra-soft / 35. ultrasonic / 36. ultra-successful / 37. ultra-thin / 38. ultra-trim / 39. ultra-violent / 40. ultra-wealthy / 41. ultra-wide / 42. umbrella-busting / 43. unable / 44. unaccented / 45. unacceptable / 46. unaccompanied / 47. unaccountable / 48. unaccounted for / 49. unaccustomed / 50. unachievable / 51. unacknowledged / 52. unacquainted / 53. unadjusted / 54. unadorned / 55. unadulterated / 56. unadventurous / 57. unaffected / 58. unaffiliated / 59. unaffordable / 60. unafraid / 61. unaided / 62. unalienable / 63. unalloyed / 64. unalterable / 65. unaltered / 66. unambiguous / 67. unanimous / 68. unannounced / 69. unanswerable / 70. unanswered / 71. unanticipated / 72. unapologetic / 73. unappealing / 74. unappetizing / 75. unappreciated / 76. unapproachable / 77. unarguable / 78. unarmed / 79. unashamed / 80. unasked / 81. unasked-for / 82. unassailable / 83. unassigned / 84. unassisted / 85. unassuming / 86. unattached / 87. unattainable / 88. unattended / 89. unattractive / 90. unauthorized / 91. unavailable / 92. unavailing / 93. unavoidable / 94. unaware / 95. unawares / 96. unbalanced / 97. unbearable / 98. unbeatable / 99. unbeaten / 100. unbecoming / 101. unbefitting / 102. unbeknown / 103. unbelievable / 104. unbelieving / 105. unbending / 106. unbiased / 107. unbidden / 108. unbleached / 109. unblemished / 110. unblinking / 111. unbounded / 112. unbowed / 113. unbreakable / 114. unbridgeable / 115. unbridled / 116. unbroken / 117. unbuttoned / 118. uncalled for / 119. uncanny / 120. uncared for / 121. uncaring / 122. uncaring / 123. unceasing / 124. uncensored / 125. uncensored / 126. unceremonious / 127. uncertain / 128. unchallengeable / 129. unchallenged / 130. unchangeable / 131. unchanged / 132. unchanging /

133. uncharacteristic / 134. uncharitable / 135. uncharted / 136. unchecked / 137. unchristian / 138. uncivilized / 139. unclaimed / 140. unclassifiable / 141. unclassified / 142. unclear / 143. unclothed / 144. uncluttered / 145. uncolored / 146. uncomfortable / 147. uncommitted / 148. uncommon / 149. uncommunicative / 150. uncompetitive / 151. uncomplaining / 152. uncompleted / 153. uncomplicated / 154. uncomplimentary / 155. uncomprehending / 156. uncompromising / 157. unconcealed / 158. unconcerned / 159. unconditional / 160. unconditioned / 161. unconfirmed / 162. uncongenial / 163. unconnected / 164. unconquerable / 165. unconscionable / 166. unconscious / 167. unconsidered / 168. unconstitutional / 169. unconstrained / 170. uncontainable / 171. uncontaminated / 172. uncontested / 173. uncontrollable / 174. uncontrolled / 175. uncontroversial / 176. unconventional / 177. unconvinced / 178. unconvincing / 179. uncooked / 180. uncooperative / 181. uncoordinated / 182. uncorrectable / 183. uncorroborated / 184. uncountable / 185. uncouth / 186. uncovered / 187. uncritical / 188. uncrowned / 189. unctuous / 190. uncultivated / 191. uncultured / 192. uncut / 193. undamaged / 194. undated / 195. undaunted / 196. undecided / 197. undeclared / 198. undefeatable / 199. undefeated / 200. undefended / 201. undefined / 202. undeletable / 203. undeliverable / 204. undemanding / 205. undemocratic / 206. undemonstrative / 207. undeniable / 208. undependable / 209. under / 210. underarm / 211. undercover / 212. underdeveloped / 213. underemployed / 214. underfed / 215. underfunded / 216. underground / 217. underhanded / 218. underinsured / 219. undermanned / 220. undernourished / 221. underpaid / 222. underprepared / 223. underpriced / 224. underprivileged / 225. under-rehearsed / 226. under-represented / 227. under-resourced / 228. under-resourced / 229. under-slept / 230. understaffed / 231. understandable / 232. understated / 233. underutilized / 234. under-utilized / 235. underwhelmed / 236. underwhelming / 237. undeserved / 238. undesirable / 239. undetectable / 240. undetected / 241. undeterred / 242. undeveloped / 243. undifferentiated / 244. undignified / 245. undiluted / 246. undiminished / 247. undisciplined / 248. undisclosed / 249. undiscovered / 250. undisguised / 251. undismayed / 252. undistinguished / 253. undisturbed / 254. undividable / 255.

undivided / **256**. undocumented / **257**. undone / **258**. undoubted / **259**. undreamed-of / **260**. undressed / **261**. undrinkable / **262**. undying / **263**. unearned / **264**. unearthly / **265**. uneasy / **266**. uneatable / **267**. uneaten / **268**. uneconomic / **269**. uneconomical / **270**. unedifying / **271**. uneducated / **272**. unelectable / **273**. unelected / **274**. unemotional / **275**. unemployable / **276**. unencumbered / **277**. unending / **278**. unendurable / **279**. unenforceable / **280**. unenviable / **281**. unequal / **282**. unequalled / **283**. unequivocal / **284**. UNESCO-protected / **285**. unethical / **286**. uneven / **287**. uneventful / **288**. unexceptionable / **289**. unexceptional / **290**. unexcitable / **291**. unexpected / **292**. unexpired / **293**. unexplainable / **294**. unexplained / **295**. unexploded / **296**. unexplored / **297**. unexpressed / **298**. unexpurgated / **299**. unfailing / **300**. unfair / **301**. unfaithful / **302**. unfamiliar / **303**. unfashionable / **304**. unfathomable / **305**. unfavorable / **306**. unfazed / **307**. unfeasible / **308**. unfeeling / **309**. unfeigned / **310**. unfenced / **311**. unfettered / **312**. unfilled / **313**. unfinished / **314**. unfit / **315**. unfitted / **316**. unfixable / **317**. unflagging / **318**. unflappable / **319**. unflattering / **320**. unflinching / **321**. unfocused / **322**. unforced / **323**. unforeseeable / **324**. unforeseen / **325**. unforgettable / **326**. unforgivable / **327**. unforgiving / **328**. unformed / **329**. unforthcoming / **330**. unfortunate / **331**. unfounded / **332**. unfriendly / **333**. unfulfilled / **334**. unfulfilling / **335**. unfunny / **336**. unfurnished / **337**. ungainly / **338**. ungenerous / **339**. ungentlemanly / **340**. unglamorous / **341**. ungodly / **342**. ungovernable / **343**. ungracious / **344**. ungrammatical / **345**. ungraspable / **346**. ungrateful / **347**. unguarded / **348**. unhappily / **349**. unhappy / **350**. unharmed / **351**. unhealthy / **352**. unheard / **353**. unheard-of / **354**. unheated / **355**. unheeded / **356**. unhelpful / **357**. unheralded / **358**. unhesitating / **359**. unhindered / **360**. unholy / **361**. unhurried / **362**. unhurt / **363**. unhygienic / **364**. unicameral / **365**. unicellular / **366**. unidentifiable / **367**. unidentified / **368**. uniform / **369**. uniformed / **370**. unilateral / **371**. unilateralist / **372**. unimaginable / **373**. unimaginative / **374**. unimpaired / **375**. unimpeachable / **376**. unimpeded / **377**. unimportant / **378**. unimpressed / **379**. unimpressive / **380**. uninflected / **381**. uninformative / **382**. uninhabitable / **383**. uninhibited / **384**. uninjured / **385**. uninspired / **386**. uninspiring / **387**. uninsurable / **388**. uninsured / **389**. unintelligent / **390**. unintelligible / **391**. unintended / **392**. unintentional / **393**. uninterested /

394. uninteresting / 395. uninterruptable / 396. uninterrupted / 397. uninvited / 398. uninviting / 399. uninvolved / 400. unique / 401. unitary / 402. united / 403. universal / 404. unjust / 405. unjustifiable / 406. unjustified / 407. unkempt / 408. unkind / 409. unknowable / 410. unknowing / 411. unknown / 412. unlawful / 413. unleaded / 414. unleavened / 415. unlettered / 416. unlicensed / 417. unlike / 418. unlikely / 419. unlimited / 420. unlined / 421. unlisted / 422. unlocked / 423. unlooked-for / 424. unlovable / 425. unloved / 426. unlovely / 427. unlucky / 428. unmade / 429. unmanageable / 430. unmanly / 431. unmanned / 432. unmannerly / 433. unmarked / 434. unmarried / 435. unmatchable / 436. unmatched / 437. unmelodious / 438. unmemorable / 439. unmentionable / 440. unmindful / 441. unmistakable / 442. unmitigated / 443. unmodified / 444. unmotivated / 445. unmoved / 446. unmoving / 447. unnamed / 448. unnatural / 449. unnecessary / 450. unnoticeable / 451. unnoticed / 452. unnumbered / 453. unobjectionable / 454. unobservable / 455. unobserved / 456. unobtainable / 457. unobtrusive / 458. unoccupied / 459. unofficial / 460. unopened / 461. unopposed / 462. unorganized / 463. unorthodox / 464. unpaid / 465. unpalatable / 466. unparalleled / 467. unpardonable / 468. unpatriotic / 469. unperturbed / 470. unplaced / 471. unplanned / 472. unplayable / 473. unpleasant / 474. unpolluted / 475. unpopular / 476. unprecedented / 477. unpredictable / 478. unprejudiced / 479. unpremeditated / 480. unprepared / 481. unpretentious / 482. unprincipled / 483. unprintable / 484. unproblematic / 485. unproductive / 486. unprofessional / 487. unprofitable / 488. unpromising / 489. unprompted / 490. unpronounceable / 491. unprotected / 492. unproven / 493. unprovoked / 494. unpublished / 495. unqualified / 496. unquantifiable / 497. unquenchable / 498. unquestionable / 499. unquestioned / 500. unquestioning / 501. unquiet / 502. unreachable / 503. unread / 504. unreadable / 505. unreal / 506. unrealistic / 507. unrealizable / 508. unrealized / 509. unreasonable / 510. unreasoning / 511. unrecognizable / 512. unrecognized / 513. unreconstructed / 514. unrecorded / 515. unrecoverable / 516. unrefined / 517. unrelenting / 518. unreliable / 519. unrelieved / 520. unremarkable / 521. unremarked / 522. unremitting / 523. unrepeatable / 524. unrepentant / 525. unreported / 526. unrepresentative / 527. unrequited / 528.

unreserved / **529.** unresolved / **530.** unresponsive / **531.** unrest-hit / **532.** unrestrained / **533.** unrestricted / **534.** unrewarded / **535.** unrewarding / **536.** unripe / **537.** unrivalled / **538.** unrounded / **539.** unruffled / **540.** unruly / **541.** unsafe / **542.** unsaid / **543.** unsalable / **544.** unsalted / **545.** unsanitary / **546.** unsatisfactory / **547.** unsatisfied / **548.** unsatisfying / **549.** unsavory / **550.** unscathed / **551.** unscheduled / **552.** unscientific / **553.** unscripted / **554.** unscrupulous / **555.** unseasonable / **556.** unseasonal / **557.** unseeded / **558.** unseeing / **559.** unseemly / **560.** unseen / **561.** unselfconscious / **562.** unselfish / **563.** unsellable / **564.** unsentimental / **565.** unserviceable / **566.** unsettled / **567.** unsettling / **568.** unshakable / **569.** unshaken / **570.** unshaven / **571.** unsightly / **572.** unsinkable / **573.** unskilled / **574.** unsmiling / **575.** unsociable / **576.** unsocial / **577.** unsold / **578.** unsolicited / **579.** unsolvable / **580.** unsolved / **581.** unsophisticated / **582.** unsorted / **583.** unsound / **584.** unsparing / **585.** unspeakable / **586.** unspecified / **587.** unspectacular / **588.** unspoiled / **589.** unspoken / **590.** unsporting / **591.** unsportsmanlike / **592.** unstable / **593.** unstated / **594.** unsteady / **595.** unstinting / **596.** unstoppable / **597.** unstressed / **598.** unstructured / **599.** unstuck / **600.** unsubstantiated / **601.** unsuccessful / **602.** unsuitable / **603.** unsuited / **604.** unsullied / **605.** unsupportable / **606.** unsupported / **607.** unsure / **608.** unsurpassable / **609.** unsurpassed / **610.** unsurprised / **611.** unsurprising / **612.** unsuspected / **613.** unsuspecting / **614.** unsustainable / **615.** unsweetened / **616.** unswerving / **617.** unsympathetic / **618.** unsystematic / **619.** untainted / **620.** untalented / **621.** untamed / **622.** untapped / **623.** untenable / **624.** untested / **625.** unthinkable / **626.** unthinking / **627.** untidy / **628.** untimely / **629.** untiring / **630.** untold / **631.** untouchable / **632.** untouched / **633.** untraceable / **634.** untrained / **635.** untrammeled / **636.** untranslatable / **637.** untreated / **638.** untried / **639.** untrue / **640.** untrustworthy / **641.** untruthful / **642.** unturned / **643.** untutored / **644.** untypical / **645.** unusable / **646.** unused / **647.** unusual / **648.** unutterable / **649.** unvarnished / **650.** unvarying / **651.** unverifiable / **652.** unvoiced / **653.** unwaged / **654.** unwanted / **655.** unwarrantable / **656.** unwarranted / **657.** unwary / **658.** unwashed / **659.** unwatchable / **660.** unwavering / **661.** unwelcome / **662.** unwelcoming / **663.** unwholesome / **664.** unwieldy / **665.** unwilling / **666.** unwinnable / **667.** unwise / **668.** unwitting / **669.** unwonted / **670.** unworkable / **671.**

unworldly / **672**. unworried / **673**. unworthy / **674**. unwritten / **675**. unyielding / **676**. up to date / **677**. up-and-coming / **678**. upbeat / **679**. upcoming / **680**. upfront / **681**. upgradable / **682**. upgradeable / **683**. uphill / **684**. uplifted / **685**. uplifting / **686**. upmost / **687**. upper / **688**. upper-caste dominated / **689**. uppermost / **690**. upraised / **691**. upright / **692**. uproarious / **693**. upscale / **694**. upset / **695**. upsetting / **696**. upstage / **697**. upstanding / **698**. uptight / **699**. up-to-the-minute / **700**. upturned / **701**. upward / **702**. urban / **703**. urban-centric / **704**. urbanized / **705**. urgent / **706**. urinary / **707**. usable / **708**. used / **709**. useful / **710**. useless / **711**. user-centric / **712**. user-friendly / **713**. user-friendly / **714**. usual / **715**. usurious / **716**. utilitarian / **717**. utility / **718**. utilizable / **719**. utmost / **720**. utopian / **721**. uttermost / **722**. uvular

02v. Useful Adjectives -- 'V'

1. vacant / 2. vacuous / 3. vague / 4. vain / 5. vainglorious / 6. valedictory / 7. valiant / 8. valid / 9. valuable / 10. value-based / 11. value-laden / 12. valueless / 13. vanilla-flavored / 14. vapid / 15. vaporous / 16. variable / 17. varied / 18. variegated / 19. various / 20. varsity / 21. vascular / 22. vast / 23. vaulted / 24. vaunted / 25. vegetal / 26. vegetarian / 27. vegetated / 28. vehement / 29. vehicle-lifter / 30. vehicular / 31. veil-draped / 32. veiled / 33. veined / 34. velvety / 35. venal / 36. venerable / 37. venereal / 38. vengeful / 39. venomous / 40. venous / 41. ventral / 42. verbal / 43. verbatim / 44. verbose / 45. verdant / 46. verifiable / 47. veritable / 48. vernacular / 49. vernal / 50. versatile / 51. vertical / 52. vertiginous / 53. vertigo-inducing / 54. very / 55. vestigial / 56. veterinary / 57. veto-wielding / 58. vexatious / 59. vexed / 60. viable / 61. vibrant / 62. vicarious / 63. vicious / 64. victimless / 65. Victorian / 66. victorious / 67. viewable / 68. vigorous / 69. vile / 70. villainous / 71. vindictive / 72. vintage / 73. violence-affected / 74. violence-drenched / 75. violence-free / 76. violence-hit / 77. violence-plagued / 78. violence-ridden / 79. violence-wrecked / 80. violent / 81. viral / 82. virgin / 83. virile / 84. virtual / 85. virtuoso / 86. virtuous / 87. virulent / 88. virus-related / 89. visceral / 90. viscid / 91. viscous / 92. visible / 93. visibly relaxed / 94. visionary / 95. vision-related / 96. visiting / 97. visual / 98. vital / 99. vitamin-rich / 100. vitreous / 101. vitriolic / 102. vivacious / 103. vivid / 104. viviparous / 105. vocal / 106. vocational / 107. vociferous / 108. voice-activated / 109. voiced / 110. voiceless / 111. void / 112. voidable / 113. volatile / 114. volcanic / 115. voluble / 116. voluminous / 117. voluntary / 118. voluptuous / 119. voracious / 120. vote-counting / 121. vote-winning / 122. vulnerable

02w. Useful Adjectives -- 'W'

1. wage-related / 2. waggish / 3. waist-deep / 4. waist-high / 5. wakeful / 6. waking / 7. walk-in / 8. walking / 9. walk-on / 10. walloping / 11. wall-to-wall / 12. wanted / 13. wanting / 14. wanton / 15. war-battered / 16. war-crippled / 17. war-devastated / 18. warlike / 19. war-like / 20. warm / 21. warm-blooded / 22. warm-hearted / 23. warped / 24. war-ravaged / 25. warring / 26. war-sapped / 27. war-stricken / 28. war-torn / 29. war-wrecked / 30. washable / 31. washed out / 32. washed up / 33. waspish / 34. waste / 35. waste-based / 36. wasted / 37. wasteful / 38. wasting / 39. watchable / 40. watchful / 41. water-borne / 42. water-cooled / 43. water-deprived / 44. water-drawing / 45. water-filled / 46. water-guzzling / 47. waterless / 48. watermelon-sized / 49. waterproof / 50. water-related / 51. water-soaked / 52. water-starved / 53. water-stressed / 54. watery / 55. watery-eyed / 56. wavy / 57. wavy-haired / 58. wayward / 59. weak / 60. weak-kneed / 61. wearable / 62. wearing / 63. weary / 64. weather-related / 65. weather-resistant / 66. web-enabled / 67. wedded / 68. wedding-related / 69. wee / 70. weeklong / 71. weekly / 72. weeping / 73. weepy / 74. weighted / 75. weightless / 76. weighty / 77. weird / 78. welcome / 79. welcoming / 80. welfare-oriented / 81. well / 82. well-adjusted / 83. well-adjusted / 84. well-advised / 85. well-advised / 86. well-appointed / 87. well-attended / 88. well-balanced / 89. well-behaved / 90. well-behaved / 91. well-born / 92. well-bred / 93. well-built / 94. well-connected / 95. well-coordinated / 96. well-cut / 97. well-defined / 98. well-designed / 99. well-developed / 100. well-disposed / 101. well-distributed / 102. well-documented / 103. well-dressed / 104. well-earned / 105. well-earned / 106. well-endowed / 107. well-entrenched / 108. well-established / 109. well-fed / 110. well-fitted / 111. well-formed / 112. well-founded / 113. well-groomed / 114. well-grounded / 115. well-guarded / 116. well-healed / 117. well-heeled / 118. well-hung / 119. well-informed / 120. well-inked / 121. well-intentioned / 122. well-kept / 123. well-known / 124. well-lit / 125. well-mannered / 126. well-matched / 127. well-meaning / 128. well-meant / 129. well-off / 130. well-oiled / 131. well-oiled / 132. well-orchestrated / 133. well-paid / 134. well-planned / 135. well-preserved / 136. well-publicized / 137. well-read / 138. well-regulated / 139. well-researched /

140. well-rounded / **141**. well-run / **142**. well-spoken / **143**. well-thought of / **144**. well-thought out / **145**. well-thumbed / **146**. well-timed / **147**. well-to-do / **148**. well-traveled / **149**. well-tried / **150**. well-trodden / **151**. well-turned / **152**. well-used / **153**. well-ventilated / **154**. well-worn / **155**. welsh / **156**. west / **157**. westerly / **158**. western / **159**. westernmost / **160**. wet / **161**. wet-clothed / **162**. whacked / **163**. whacking / **164**. whale-sized / **165**. wheezy / **166**. whirlwind / **167**. whiskered / **168**. whistle-stop / **169**. white / **170**. white-beaked / **171**. white-bread / **172**. white-helmeted / **173**. white-hot / **174**. whitish / **175**. whole / **176**. wholehearted / **177**. wholesale / **178**. wholesome / **179**. wicked / **180**. wide / **181**. wide-eyed / **182**. widely acclaimed / **183**. widely anticipated / **184**. widely circulated / **185**. widely debated / **186**. widely expected / **187**. widely held / **188**. widely published / **189**. widely revered / **190**. widely reviled / **191**. wide-ranging / **192**. wide-ranging / **193**. widespread / **194**. wifely / **195**. Wi-Fi-enabled / **196**. wiggly / **197**. wild / **198**. wildcat / **199**. wildlife-related / **200**. wiling / **201**. willful / **202**. wilted / **203**. wily / **204**. wind-driven / **205**. windless / **206**. windowless / **207**. wind-powered / **208**. wind-scoured / **209**. windswept / **210**. wind-up / **211**. windward / **212**. windy / **213**. winged / **214**. wingless / **215**. winnable / **216**. winning / **217**. win-oriented / **218**. winsome / **219**. wintry / **220**. wireless / **221**. wiry / **222**. wise / **223**. wishy-washy / **224**. wistful / **225**. withdrawn / **226**. withered / **227**. withering / **228**. witless / **229**. wittingly / **230**. witty / **231**. wizened / **232**. wobbly / **233**. womanish / **234**. womanly / **235**. women-centric / **236**. women-dominated / **237**. women-oriented / **238**. women-owned / **239**. women-related / **240**. wonder-filled / **241**. wonderful / **242**. wondrous / **243**. wonky / **244**. wont / **245**. wooded / **246**. wooden / **247**. woodsy / **248**. woody / **249**. woolen / **250**. woolly / **251**. wordless / **252**. wordy / **253**. workable / **254**. workaday / **255**. working / **256**. workless / **257**. work-related / **258**. work-shy / **259**. worldly-wise / **260**. world-renowned / **261**. worldwide / **262**. worm-infested / **263**. wormy / **264**. worried / **265**. worrying / **266**. worshipful / **267**. worst-case / **268**. worst-ever / **269**. worst-hit / **270**. worst-performing / **271**. worthless / **272**. worthwhile / **273**. worthy / **274**. wounded / **275**. wound-inflicted / **276**. wounding / **277**. wrap-around / **278**. wrapped / **279**. wreath-laying / **280**. wrecked / **281**. wretched / **282**. wringing wet / **283**. wrinkled / **284**. wrinkly / **285**. wrong / **286**. wrongful / **287**. wrong-headed

02x. Useful Adjectives -- 'XYZ'

1. year-long / 2. yellow / 3. yellow-beaked / 4. yellow-cheeked / 5. yellowish / 6. yesterday / 7. yielding / 8. young / 9. youngish / 10. youthful / 11. yo-yo / 12. zealous / 13. zoological

02. <u>Types</u> of <u>Adjectives</u>

1. **Descriptive Adjectives**
2. **Quantitative Adjectives**
3. **Demonstrative Adjectives**
4. **Possessive Adjectives**
5. **Interrogative Adjectives**
6. **Distributive Adjectives**
7. **Article Adjectives**

1. DESCRIPTIVE ADJECTIVES

Descriptive adjectives are used to describe nouns and pronouns. Some descriptive adjectives are as follows:
Attractive / Charming / Intelligent / Polite / Small / Sour

Example Sentences:
He lives in a **small** *house.*
He is a **polite** *person.*

2. QUANTITATIVE ADJECTIVES

Quantitative adjectives describe the quantity of something. Some quantitative adjectives are as follows:
One / Two / Many / Half / Double / Hundred / Million / Billions

Example Sentences:
I have only **one** *car.*
He has **two** *houses.*
Many *students* are absent today.
Half *glass* is empty.
It may even cost **double** *the amount.*

3. DEMONSTRATIVE ADJECTIVES

A demonstrative adjective describes "which" noun or pronoun you're referring to. These adjectives are as follows:

This -- used to refer to a singular noun close to you.
These -- used to refer to a plural noun close to you.
That -- used to refer to a singular noun far from you.
Those -- used to refer to a plural noun far from you.

Example Sentences:
This *song* is melodious.
These *songs* are melodious.
That *shop* is closed.
Those *shops* are closed.

4. POSSESSIVE ADJECTIVES

Possessive adjectives describe to whom a thing belongs. These adjectives are as follows:

My (the possessive form of 'I') -- of or belonging to me
His (the possessive form of 'He') -- of or belonging to him
Her (the possessive form of 'Her') -- of or belonging to her
Their (the possessive form of 'They') -- of or belonging to them
Your (the possessive form of 'You') -- of or belonging to you
Our (the possessive form of 'We') -- of or belonging to us

Example Sentences:
This is **my** *computer.*
This is **his** *computer.*
This is **her** *computer.*
This is **their** *computer.*
This is **your** *computer.*
This is **our** *computer.*

You can also use the following possessives adjectives if you want to leave off the noun or pronoun being modified: **Mine / His / Hers / Theirs / Yours / Ours**

Example Sentences:
This is **mine.**
This is **his.**
This is **hers.**
This is **theirs.**
This is **yours.**
This is **ours.**

5. INTERROGATIVE ADJECTIVES

Interrogative adjectives are immediately followed by a noun or a pronoun, and are used to form questions. The interrogative adjectives are as follows:

Which -- used to ask to make a choice between options
What -- used to ask to make a choice in general
Whose -- used to ask who something belongs to

Example Sentences:

Which movie would you like to watch? ('movie' is a noun)
Which person do you most agree with? ('person' is a noun)
Which subject is right for him? ('subject' is a noun)

What career do you dream of? ('career' is a noun)
What post does he hold? ('post' is a noun)
What impact has the education had on your daughter? ('impact' is a noun)

Whose fault is it anyway? ('fault' is a noun)

Whose speech is good and whose is bad? ('speech' is a noun)

6. DISTRIBUTIVE ADJECTIVES

Distributive adjectives are used to single out one or more individual items or people. Some of the most common distributive adjectives are as follows:

Any -- one of a number of things or people
Each -- every one of two or more people or things
Every -- all the members of a group of things or people
Either -- one or the other of two
Neither -- not one nor the other of two things or people

Example Sentences:
Take **any** *pen* you like.
Each *match* from the first round itself was very tough.
Every *life* counts.
"Which of these two bicycles would you buy?" "**Either** (bicycle) will do."
Neither of us has/have laptop.

7. ARTICLE ADJECTIVES

Articles are actually adjectives because they describe the nouns that they precede. In English, there are only three articles: **the, a, and an.**

Example Sentences:
A *student* was forced to leave the college on account of indiscipline.
I eat **an** *egg* every day.
The *complainant* was asked to produce the evidence to substantiate the charges.

03. <u>Degrees</u> of <u>Adjectives</u>

"Degrees of Adjectives" refers to adjectives being written in different forms to compare one or more persons, places, things or events.

There Are Three Degrees of Adjectives

Positive Degree -- Positive degree denotes a normal adjective that is used to describe, or there is comparison of equality or inequality.
Example Sentences:
She is **emotional.** (No Comparison)
She is **as emotional as** her sister. (Comparison of equality)
She is **not as/so emotional as** her sister. (Comparison of Inequality)

Comparative Degree -- Comparative degree denotes an adjective that is used to compare two things (and is often followed by the word than or to).
Example Sentences:
She is **more emotional** than her sister.
I am **younger** to him.

Superlative Degree -- Superlative degree denotes an adjective that is used to compare three or more things, or to state that something is the most.
Example Sentences:
She is the **most emotional** girl of our class.
He is the **smartest boy** in my family.

You can place **-er** and **-est** in front of many adjectives in order to create Comparative and Superlative forms. You can use this method for making comparative and superlative forms of the *adjectives with one syllable or adjectives with two syllables ending in --y, --er, --le, --ow*

Positive -- Comparative -- Superlative

001. black -- black**er** -- black**est**
002. blind -- blind**er** -- blind**est**
003. blunt -- blunt**er** -- blunt**est**
004. bold -- bold**er** -- bold**est**
005. brief -- brief**er** -- brief**est**
006. bright -- bright**er** -- bright**est**
007. broad -- broad**er** -- broad**est**
008. brown -- brown**er** -- brown**est**
009. calm -- calm**er** -- calm**est**
010. cheap -- cheap**er** -- cheap**est**
011. clean -- clean**er** -- clean**est**
012. clear -- clear**er** -- clear**est**
013. clever -- clev**erer** -- clev**erest**
014. cold -- cold**er** -- cold**est**
015. common -- common**er** -- common**est**
016. cool -- cool**er** -- cool**est**
017. crisp -- crispi**er** -- crispi**est**
018. cruel -- cruel**er** -- cruel**est**
019. daft -- daft**er** -- daft**est**
020. damp -- damp**er** -- damp**est**
021. dark -- dark**er** -- dark**est**
022. deaf -- deaf**er** -- deaf**est**
023. dear -- dear**er** -- dear**est**
024. deep -- deep**er** -- deep**est**
025. dull -- dull**er** -- dull**est**
026. dumb -- dumb**er** -- dumb**est**
027. faint -- faint**er** -- faint**est**
028. fair -- fair**er** -- fair**est**
029. fast -- fast**er** -- fast**est**
030. firm -- firm**er** /firm**est**
031. fond -- fond**er** -- fond**est**
32. foul -- foul**er** -- foul**est**
033. frail -- frail**er** -- frail**est**
034. frank -- frank**er** -- frank**est**
035. fresh -- fresh**er** -- fresh**est**
036. full -- full**er** -- full**est**

037. gory -- gorier -- goriest
038. grand -- grander -- grandest
039. great -- greater -- greatest
040. green -- greener -- greenest
041. gross -- grosser /grossest
042. hard -- harder -- hardest
043. harsh -- harsher -- harshest
044. high -- higher -- highest
045. kind -- kinder -- kindest
046. light -- lighter -- lightest
047. little -- smaller -- smallest
048. long -- longer -- longest
049. loud -- louder -- loudest
050. low -- lower -- lowest
051. mean -- meaner -- meanest
052. meek -- meeker -- meekest
053. mellow -- mellower -- mellowest
054. mild -- milder -- mildest
055. narrow -- narrower -- narrowest
056. near -- nearer -- nearest
057. neat -- neater -- neatest
058. new -- newer -- newest
059. odd -- odder -- oddest
060. old -- older -- oldest
061. plain -- plainer -- plainest
062. plump -- plumper -- plumpest
063. poor -- poorer -- poorest
064. prim -- primmer -- primmest
065. proud -- prouder -- proudest
066. queer -- queerer -- queerest
067. quick -- quicker -- quickest
068. rich -- richer -- richest
069. round -- rounder -- roundest
070. shallow -- shallower -- shallowest
071. sharp -- sharper -- sharpest
072. short -- shorter -- shortest

073. shrewd -- shrewder -- shrewdest

074. shrill -- shriller -- shrillest

075. slack -- slacker -- slackest

076. sleek -- sleeker -- sleekest

077. slender -- slenderer -- slenderest

078. slick -- slicker -- slickest

079. slick -- slicker -- slickest

080. slight -- slighter -- slightest

081. slow -- slower -- slowest

082. small -- smaller -- smallest

083. smart -- smarter -- smartest

84. smooth -- smoother -- smoothest

085. soft -- softer -- softest

086. sound -- sounder -- soundest

087. stark -- starker -- starkest

088. steep -- steeper -- steepest

089. steep -- steeper -- steepest

090. stern -- sterner -- sternest

091. stiff -- stiffer -- stiffest

092. stout -- stouter -- stoutest

093. straight -- straighter -- straightest

094. strict -- stricter -- strictest

095. strong -- stronger -- strongest

096. sweet -- sweeter -- sweetest

097. swift -- swifter -- swiftest

098. tall -- taller -- tallest

099. thick -- thicker -- thickest

100. tight -- tighter -- tightest

101. tough -- tougher -- toughest

102. warm -- warmer -- warmest

103. weak -- weaker -- weakest

104. weird -- weirder -- weirdest

105. wild -- wilder -- wildest

106. yellow -- yellower -- yellowiest

107. young -- younger -- youngest

NOTE: Spelling of the adjectives using the endings -er/-est

(a). Double the consonant after short vowel

Positive -- Comparative -- Superlative

01. big -- bigger -- biggest

02. dim -- dimmer -- dimmest

03. drab -- drabber -- drabbest

04. fat -- fatter -- fattest

05. fit -- fitter -- fittest

06. flat -- flatter -- flattest

07. hot -- hotter -- hottest

08. grim -- grimmer -- grimmest

09. hip -- hipper -- hippest

10. mad -- madder -- maddest

11. red -- redder -- reddest

12. sad -- sadder -- saddest

13. slim -- slimmer -- slimmest

14. thin -- thinner -- thinnest

15. wet -- wetter -- wettest

(b). Removing the final 'y' (if there is consonant before 'y') and adding 'ier' and 'iest'

Positive -- Comparative -- Superlative

001. angry -- angrier -- angriest

002. baggy -- baggier -- baggiest

003. beefy -- beefier -- beefiest

004. bitty -- bittier -- bittiest

005. bloody -- bloodier -- bloodiest

006. boggy -- boggier -- boggiest

007. bonny -- bonnier -- bonniest

008. bony -- bonier -- boniest

009. bossy -- bossier -- bossiest

010. bouncy -- bouncier -- bounciest

011. brainy -- brainer -- brainiest

012. bubbly -- bubblier -- bubbliest

013. bulky -- bulkier -- bulkiest

014. bumpy -- bumpier -- bumpiest

015. bushy -- bushi**er** -- bushi**est**

016. bushy -- bushi**er** -- bushi**est**

017. busy -- busi**er** -- busi**est**

018. cagey -- cagi**er** -- cagi**est**

019. catchy -- catchi**er** -- catchi**est**

020. chatty -- chatti**er** -- chatti**est**

021. cheeky -- cheeki**er** -- cheeki**est**

022. cheery -- che**erier** -- che**eriest**

023. cheesy -- cheesi**er** -- cheesi**est**

024. chewy -- chewi**er** -- chewi**est**

025. chilly -- chilli**er** -- chilli**est**

026. choosy -- choosi**er** -- choosi**est**

027. chubby -- chubbi**er** -- chubbi**est**

028. chunky -- chunki**er** -- chunki**est**

029. clammy -- clammi**er** -- clammi**est**

030. classy -- classi**er** -- classi**est**

031. cloudy -- cloudi**er** -- cloudi**est**

032. clumsy -- clumsi**er** -- clumsi**est**

033. cocky -- cocki**er** -- cocki**est**

034. comfy -- comfi**er** -- comfi**est**

035. costly -- costli**er** -- costli**est**

036. cozy -- cozi**er** -- cozi**est**

037. crafty -- crafti**er** -- crafti**est**

038. crazy -- crazi**er** -- crazi**est**

039. creamy -- creami**er** -- creami**est**

040. cruddy -- cruddi**er** -- cruddi**est**

041. crusty -- crusti**er** -- crusti**est**

042. cushy -- cushi**er** -- cushi**est**

043. daffy -- daffi**er** -- daffi**est**

044. dainty -- dainti**er** -- dainti**est**

045. deadly -- deadli**er** -- deadli**est**

046. dingy -- dingi**er** -- dingi**est**

047. dirty -- dirti**er** -- dirti**est**

048. dotty -- dotti**er** -- dotti**est**

049. dowdy -- dowdi**er** -- dowdi**est**

050. dreamy -- dreami**er** -- dreami**est**

051. dressy -- dressier -- dressiest
052. drippy -- drippier -- drippiest
053. drowsy -- drowsier -- drowsiest
054. dry -- drier -- driest
055. ducky -- duckier -- duckiest
056. early -- earlier -- earliest
057. earthy -- earthier -- earthiest
058. easy -- easier -- easiest
059. edgy -- edgier -- edgiest
060. empty -- emptier -- emptiest
061. fancy -- fancier -- fanciest
062. fatty -- fattier -- fattiest
063. feisty -- feistier -- feistiest
064. filthy -- filthier -- filthiest
065. fishy -- fishier -- fishiest
066. fizzy -- fizzier -- fizziest
067. flabby -- flabbier -- flabbiest
068. flashy -- flashier -- flashiest
069. flimsy -- flimsier -- flimsiest
070. floppy -- floppier -- floppiest
071. fluffy -- fluffier -- fluffiest
072. foggy -- foggier -- foggiest
073. friendly -- -- friendlier -- friendliest
074. frisky -- friskier -- friskiest
075. fruity -- fruitier -- fruitiest
076. funky -- funkier -- funkiest
077. funny -- funnier -- funniest
078. furry -- furrier -- furriest
079. fussy -- fussier -- fussiest
080. fuzzy -- fuzzier -- fuzziest
081. ghastly -- ghastlier -- ghastliest
082. ghostly -- ghostlier -- ghostliest
083. giddy -- giddier -- giddiest
084. giddy -- giddier -- giddiest
085. glassy -- glassier -- glassiest
086. gloomy -- gloomier -- gloomiest

087. glossy -- glossier -- glossiest
088. grainy -- grainier -- grainiest
089. grassy -- grassier -- grassiest
090. greasy -- greasier -- greasiest
091. greedy -- greedier -- greediest
092. gritty -- grittier -- grittiest
093. groggy -- groggier -- groggiest
094. grubby -- grubbier -- grubbiest
095. grumpy -- grumpier -- grumpiest
096. guilty -- guiltier -- guiltiest
097. hairy -- hairier -- hairiest
098. hammy -- hammier -- hammiest
099. handy -- handier -- handiest
100. happy -- happier -- happiest
101. hardy -- hardier -- hardiest
102. hasty -- hastier -- hastiest
103. haughty -- haughtier -- haughtiest
104. hazy -- hazier -- haziest
105. heady -- headier -- headiest
106. healthy -- healthier -- healthiest
107. hearty -- heartier -- heartiest
108. heavy -- heavier -- heaviest
109. hefty -- heftier -- heftiest
110. hilly -- hillier -- hilliest
111. holy -- holier -- holiest
112. homely -- homelier -- homeliest
113. hungry -- hungrier -- hungriest
114. husky -- huskier -- huskiest
115. icy -- icier -- iciest
116. jolly -- jollier -- jolliest
117. juicy -- juicier -- juiciest
118. knotty -- knottier -- knottiest
119. lanky -- lankier -- lankiest
120. lazy -- lazier -- laziest
121. leafy -- leafier -- leafiest
122. lengthy -- lengthier -- lengthiest

123. lively -- livelier -- liveliest
124. lofty -- loftier -- loftiest
125. lonely -- lonelier -- loneliest
126. lousy -- lousier -- lousiest
127. lovely -- lovelier -- loveliest
128. lowly -- lowlier -- lowliest
129. lucky -- luckier -- luckiest
130. meaty -- meatier -- meatiest
131. merry -- merrier -- merriest
132. messy -- messier -- messiest
133. mighty -- mightier -- mightiest
134. moody -- moodier -- moodiest
135. muddy -- muddier -- muddiest
136. murky -- murkier -- murkiest
137. mushy -- mushier -- mushiest
138. musty -- mustier -- mustiest
139. naughty -- naughtier -- naughtiest
140. needy -- needier -- neediest
141. noisy -- noisier -- noisiest
142. oily -- oilier -- oiliest
143. peppy -- peppier -- peppiest
144. phony -- phonier -- phoniest
145. plucky -- pluckier -- pluckiest
146. pretty -- prettier -- prettiest
147. pricey -- pricier -- priciest
148. prickly -- pricklier -- prickliest
149. puffy -- puffier -- puffiest
150. punchy -- punchier -- punchiest
151. puny -- punier -- puniest
152. pushy -- pushier -- pushiest
153. rainy -- rainier -- rainiest
154. ready -- readier -- readiest
155. risky -- riskier -- riskiest
156. roomy -- roomier -- roomiest
157. rosy -- rosier -- rosiest
158. rowdy -- rowdier -- rowdiest

159. runny -- runnier -- runniest
160. salty -- saltier -- saltiest
161. sandy -- sandier -- sandiest
162. sappy -- sappier -- sappiest
163. sassy -- sassier -- sassiest
164. saucy -- saucier -- sauciest
165. savvy -- savvier -- savviest
166. scaly -- scalier -- scaliest
167. scanty -- scantier -- scantiest
168. scraggy -- scraggier -- scraggiest
169. scrappy -- scrappier -- scrappiest
170. scratchy -- scratchier -- scratchiest
171. scrawny -- scrawnier -- scrawniest
172. scruffy -- scruffier -- scruffiest
173. seamy -- seamier -- seamiest
174. seedy -- seedier -- seediest
175. shabby -- shabbier -- shabbiest
176. shady -- shadier -- shadiest
177. shaggy -- shaggier -- shaggiest
178. shaky -- shakier -- shakiest
179. shifty -- shiftier -- shiftiest
180. shiny -- shiner -- shiniest
181. shoddy -- shoddier -- shoddiest
182. shy -- shyer -- shyest
183. sickly -- sicklier -- sickliest
184. silky -- silkier -- silkiest
185. silly -- sillier -- silliest
186. sketchy -- sketchier -- sketchiest
187. skimpy -- skimpier -- skimpiest
188. skinny -- skinnier -- skinniest
189. sleazy -- sleazier -- sleaziest
190. sleepy -- sleepier -- sleepiest
191. slimy -- slimier -- slimiest
192. slinky -- slinkier -- slinkiest
193. sloppy -- sloppier -- sloppiest
194. slouchy -- slouchier -- slouchiest

195. smarmy -- smarmier -- smarmiest
196. smelly -- smellier -- smelliest
197. smoky -- smokier -- smokiest
198. snappy -- snappier -- snappiest
199. snazzy -- snazzier -- snazziest
200. sneaky -- sneakier -- sneakiest
201. snotty -- snottier -- snottiest
202. soggy -- soggier -- soggiest
203. soppy -- soppier -- soppiest
204. speedy -- speedier -- speediest
205. spicy -- spicier -- spiciest
206. splashy -- splashier -- splashiest
207. spooky -- spookier -- spookiest
208. sporty -- sportier -- sportiest
209. steady -- steadier -- steadiest
210. steamy -- steamier -- steamiest
211. sticky -- stickier -- stickiest
212. stingy -- stingier -- stingiest
213. stocky -- stockier -- stockiest
214. stony -- stonier -- stoniest
215. stormy -- stormier -- stormiest
216. stuffy -- stuffier -- stuffiest
217. sturdy -- sturdier -- sturdiest
218. sultry -- sultrier -- sultriest
219. sunny -- sunnier -- sunniest
220. swanky -- swankier -- swankiest
221. tacky -- tackier -- tackiest
222. tasty -- tastier -- tastiest
223. teeny -- teenier -- teeniest
224. thirsty -- thirstier -- thirstiest
225. thorny -- thornier -- thorniest
226. tidy -- tidier -- tidiest
227. tiny -- tinier -- tiniest
228. touchy -- touchier -- touchiest
229. trashy -- trashier -- trashiest
230. trendy -- trendier -- trendiest

231. tricky -- trickier -- trickiest

232. ugly -- uglier -- ugliest

233. unlucky -- unluckier -- unluckiest

234. untidy -- untidier -- untidiest

235. wavy -- wavier -- waviest

236. wealthy -- wealthier -- wealthiest

237. weary -- wearier -- weariest

238. wily -- wilier -- wiliest

239. windy -- windier -- windiest

240. witty -- wittier -- wittiest

241. worthy -- worthier -- worthiest

Exception: The words which end in 'y' preceded by a vowel do not change their spelling. In those words, you should simply add '-er' or '-est' in comparative and superlative forms respectively. (e.g. sh**y** / sh**y**er / sh**y**est).

(c). drop the silent --e at the end of the adjective
Positive -- Comparative -- Superlative

01. able -- abler -- ablest

02. bare -- barer -- barest

03. base -- baser -- basest

04. brave -- braver -- bravest

05. choice -- choicer -- choicest

06. close -- closer -- closest

07. coarse -- coarser -- coarsest

08. crude -- cruder -- crudest

09. cute -- cuter -- cutest

10. dense -- denser -- densest

11. dire -- direr -- direst

12. fine -- finer -- finest

13. gentle -- gentler -- gentlest

14. grave -- graver -- gravest

15. handsome -- handsomer -- handsomest

16. humble -- humbler -- humblest

17. white -- whiter -- whitest

18. large -- larger -- largest

19. loose -- looser -- loosest

20. Late -- Later -- Latest

21. nice -- nicer -- nicest

22. noble -- nobler -- noblest

23. pale -- paler -- palest

24. pure -- purer -- purest

25. rare -- rarer /rarest

26. remote -- remoter -- remotest

27. ripe -- riper -- ripest

28. rude -- ruder -- rudest

29. safe -- safer -- safest

30. sane -- saner -- sanest

31. scarce -- scarcer -- scarcest

32. severe -- severer -- severest

33. strange -- stranger -- strangest

34. subtle -- subtler -- subtlest

35. sure -- surer -- surest

36. tame -- tamer -- tamest

37. true -- truer -- truest

38. vague -- vaguer -- vaguest

39. vile -- viler -- vilest

40. wide -- wider -- widest

41. wise -- wiser -- wisest

B: Comparison with 'more' and 'most' -- You can use this method for making comparative and superlative forms of all adjectives with three or more syllables. You can also use this method for making comparative and superlative forms of the adjectives with two syllables (except some adjectives with two syllables ending in --y, --er, --le, --ow).

Positive -- Comparative -- Superlative

01. alert -- more alert -- most alert

02. absurd -- more absurd -- most absurd

02. ancient -- more ancient -- most ancient

03. attractive -- more attractive -- most attractive

04. beautiful -- more beautiful -- most beautiful

04. bitter -- more bitter -- most bitter

05. brilliant -- more brilliant -- most brilliant

06. careful -- more careful -- most careful

07. careless -- more careless -- most careless

08. challenging -- more challenging -- most challenging

09. cheerful -- more cheerful -- most cheerful

10. confident -- more confident -- most confident

11. courageous -- more courageous -- most courageous

12. cunning -- more cunning -- most cunning

13. dangerous -- more dangerous -- most dangerous

14. delicious -- more delicious -- most delicious

15. difficult -- more difficult -- most difficult

16. debatable -- more debatable -- most debatable

17. expensive -- more expensive -- most expensive

18. faithful -- more faithful -- most faithful

19. famous -- more famous -- most famous

20. foolish -- more foolish -- most foolish

21. forgetful -- more forgetful -- most forgetful

22. frightening -- more frightening -- most frightening

23. generous -- more generous -- most generous

24. hazardous -- more hazardous -- most hazardous

25. helpful -- more helpful -- most helpful

26. ignorant -- more ignorant -- most ignorant

27. important -- more important -- most important

28. intelligent -- more intelligent -- most intelligent

29. interesting -- more interesting -- most interesting

30. painful -- more painful -- most painful

31. popular -- more popular -- most popular

32. proper -- more proper -- most proper

33. prosperous -- more prosperous -- most prosperous

34. reckless -- more reckless -- most reckless

35. sensible -- more sensible -- most sensible

36. serious -- more serious -- most serious

37. sour -- more sour -- most sour

38. splendid -- more splendid -- most splendid
39. terrible -- more terrible -- most terrible
40. thoughtful -- more thoughtful -- most thoughtful
41. unusual -- more unusual -- most unusual
42. useful -- more useful -- most useful
43. valuable -- more valuable -- most valuable
44. wonderful -- more wonderful -- most wonderful
45. zealous -- more zealous -- most zealous

C: Comparison by using different words -- Some adjectives make their comparative and superlative forms by using different words entirely (such as "good, better, best").

Positive -- Comparative -- Superlative
01. Bad -- Worse -- Worst
02. Good -- Better -- Best
03. Little -- Less -- Least
04. Many -- More -- Most
05. Much -- More -- Most
06. Well -- Better / Best

D: Special adjectives -- Some adjectives have two possible forms of comparison (-er/est and more/most).

Positive -- Comparative | Superlative
01. *clever* -- cleverer / more clever | cleverest / most clever
02. *common* -- commoner / more common | commonest / most common
03. *feeble* -- feebler / more feeble | feeblest / most feeble
04. *funny* -- funnier / more funny | funniest / most funny
05. *gentle* -- gentler / more gentle | gentlest / most gentle
06. *handsome* -- handsomer / more handsome | handsomest / most handsome
07. *likely* -- likelier / more likely | likeliest / most likely
08. *narrow* -- narrower / more narrow | narrowest / most narrow

09. *pleasant* -- pleasanter / more pleasant | pleasantest / most pleasant
10. *polite* -- politer / more polite | politest / most polite
11. *quiet* -- quieter / more quiet | quietest / most quiet
12. *simple* -- simpler / more simple | simplest / most simple
13. *sorry* -- sorrier / more sorry | sorriest / most sorry
14. *stupid* -- stupidier / more stupid | stupidiest / most stupid
15. *subtle* -- subtler / more subtle | subtlest / most subtle

E: No Comparative Form -- Some adjectives have only superlative forms.

Positive -- Comparative | Superlative
01. minute -- **N/A** -- minut**est**
02. sincere -- **N/A** -- sincer**est**
03. staunch -- **N/A** -- staunch**est**

<u>Adjectives That Don't Have The Comparative Or The Superlative Forms</u>

absolute / adequate / chief / complete / entire / eternal / final / ideal / impossible / inevitable / irrevocable / main / manifest / minor / paramount / perfect / preferable / principal / rectangular / round / square / stationary / sufficient / unanimous / unavoidable / unbroken / unique / universal / whole, etc.

04. Formation of Adjectives

An adjective can be a single word (like affordable, rough) or a compound (awe-inspiring, clear-headed) that actually modifies the noun.

04a. Using 'Prefixes and Suffixes'

(A1). FORMATION OF ADJECTIVES USING SUFFIXES

Many adjectives are created by adding prefixes and suffixes to nouns, verbs and even other adjectives. Prefixes go at the beginning of words while Suffixes go on the end of words. They can change a word from one part of speech, such as a noun or a verb, to another, such as an adjective. For example, if you add '-ful' to 'play', you create the adjective 'playful'. If you add '-less' to 'age', you create the adjective 'ageless'.

Common suffixes that are used to create adjectives:-

01. -able (meaning: ability, possibility) --
Examples: allow**able**, eat**able**, practic**able**

02. -an (meaning: typical of, native of) --
Examples: Afric**an**, Americ**an**, Germ**an**

03. -ant (meaning: having the characteristic of) --
Examples: assist**ant**, ignor**ant**, reli**ant**

04. -al (meaning: having the quality/characteristic/relation of) --
Examples: anecdot**al**, architectur**al**, function**al**, tradition**al**
General Spelling rule (Add '-al' as a suffix. If ending with an 'e', remove it and add 'al'. (nature -- natur**al**)

05. -ary (meaning: having the quality or characteristic of; related to) --
Examples: caution**ary**, disciplin**ary**, vision**ary**
General Spelling rule (Add '-ary' as a suffix. If ending with an 'e', remove it. (discipline -- disciplin**ary**)

06. -ed (meaning: having the quality of) --
Examples: absorb**ed**, motivat**ed**, terrifi**ed**

07. -ent (meaning: having the characteristic of) --
Examples: benefic**ent**, compet**ent**, depend**ent**

08. -ful (meaning: having the characteristic of) --
Examples: boast**ful**, care**ful**, doubt**ful**
General Spelling rule (Add '-ful' as a suffix. If ending with 'ty', replace it with 'i'. (plenty -- plenti**ful**)

09. -ial (meaning: having the quality/characteristic/relation of) --
Examples: adverb**ial**, manager**ial**, substant**ial**

10. -ian (meaning: typical of; related to) --
Examples: civil**ian**, humanitar**ian**, Victor**ian**

11. -ible (meaning: ability, possibility) --
Examples: access**ible**, digest**ible**, permiss**ible**

12. -ic (meaning: having the quality of) --
Examples: algebra**ic**, alphabet**ic**, parasit**ic**

13. -ical (meaning: having the quality/characteristic/relation of) --
Examples: analyt**ical**, histor**ical**, statist**ical**

14. -ing (meaning: refereeing to an activity) --
Examples: appeal**ing**, match**ing**, press**ing**

15. -ish (meaning: having the characteristic of; native of; approximately or somewhat) --
Examples: book**ish**, child**ish**, green**ish**
General Spelling rule (Add '-ish' as a suffix (girl -- girl**ish**)

16. -ive (meaning: having the quality of) --
Examples: alternat**ive**, collect**ive**, contemplat**ive**,

General Spelling rule (Add '-ive' as a suffix. -If ending with an 'e', remove it. -If ending with 'ion', remove it. (contemplate -- contempla**tive,** prescription -- prescrip**tive**)

17. -less (meaning: without) --
Examples: driver**less**, end**less**, need**less**
General Spelling rule (Add '-less' as a suffix. If ending with a 'y', replace it with 'i'. (emotion -- emotion**less,** penny -- penni**less**)

18. -ly (meaning: in a way that is mentioned) --
Examples: kind**ly**, time**ly**
General Spelling rule (Add '-ly' as a suffix. (time -- time**ly**)

19. -ous (meaning: having the characteristic or nature of) --
Examples: advantage**ous**, nitrogen**ous**, poison**ous**
General Spelling rule (Add '-ous' as a suffix. -If ending with an 'e', remove it. If ending with a 'y', replace it with 'i', -If ending with 'cle', replace it with 'cul' (fame -- fam**ous**, mystery -- mysteri**ous**, miracle -- miracul**ous**)

20. -some (likely or apt to) --
Examples: loath**some,** trouble**some**

21. -y (meaning: having the action, characteristic or process of) --
Examples: cloud**y**, need**y**, storm**y**

(A2). FORMATION OF ADJECTIVES USING PREFIXES

Common prefixes that are used to create adjectives:-

01. dis- (meaning: not or opposite of) --
Examples: **dis**loyal, **dis**consolate, **dis**interested

02. hyper- (meaning: over, beyond, above) --
Examples: **hyper**active, **hyper**sensitive, **hyper**critical

03. il- (meaning: not or opposite of) --

Examples: Illegal, Illegible, Illogical
General Spelling rule (Add 'il-' as a prefix for words starting with 'i'. (logical -- illogical, legible -- illegible)

04. im- (meaning: not or opposite of) --
Examples: Immature, Immoral, Impatient
General Spelling rule (Add 'im-' as a prefixes for words starting with 'm' or 'p'. (moral -- immoral, impatient -- impatient)

05. in- (meaning: not or opposite of, lacking) --
Examples: Inaccurate, Inattentive, Incomplete

06. inter- (meaning: between, not within) --
Examples: **inter**active, **inter**cultural, **inter**dependent

07. ir- (meaning: not or opposite of) --
Examples: Irrecoverable, Irreligious, Irreversible
General Spelling rule (Add 'ir-' as a prefixes for words starting with 'r' (religious -- irreligious, reversible -- irreversible).

08. super- (meaning: extreme) --
Examples: **super**natural, **super**script, **super**-sized

09. trans- (meaning: across) --
Examples: **trans**atlantic, **trans**gender, **trans**national

10. un- (meaning: not or opposite of) --
Examples: **un**afraid, **un**aware, **un**certain

11. ultra- (meaning: extreme) --
Examples: **ultra**-high, **ultra**-thin, **ultra**-sensitive

04b. Using 'Combining Forms'

Combining form is a form of a word that can combine with free word, root word or another combining form to get a new word. 'Combining form' adds extra meaning to the new word. 'Combining form' is added to the beginning or end of free word, root word or another combining form. Many adjectives are created by adding **combining form** to other words. Many words ending in "**-ing**", "**-ed**", "**-en**", etc. are used as **COMBINING FORMS**.

EXAMPLES:

Formation of Adjectives Using Combining Form '-AFFECTED'
General meaning: suffering from the thing that is mentioned
ADJECTIVES: cyclone-**affected** / drought-**affected** / drug-**affected** / explosion-**affected** / famine-**affected** / flood-**affected** / flu-**affected** / militancy-**affected** / quake-**affected** / rain-**affected** / violence-**affected**

Formation of Adjectives Using Combining Form '-BASED'
General meaning: containing something as an important feature or part
ADJECTIVES: agri-**based** / animal-**based** / app-**based** / bio-**based** / browser-**based** / carbon-**based** / cash-**based** / caste-**based** / census-**based** / city-**based** / computer-**based** / data-**based** / demand-**based** / district-**based** / education-**based** / evidence-**based** / factor-**based** / faith-**based** / foreign-**based** / home-**based** / income-**based** / Internet-**based** / issue-**based** / light-**based** / location-**based** / merit-**based** / outcome-**based** / performance-**based** / petroleum-**based** / religion-**based** / risk-**based** / robot-**based** / server-**based** / sports-**based** / test-**based** / value-**based** / web-**based**

Formation of Adjectives Using Combining Form '-LONG' / 'LONG-'
General meaning: length of time, distance, object, etc.
ADJECTIVES: day-**long** / decades-**long** / foot-**long** / hour-**long** / life-**long** / week-**long** / **long**-awaited / **long**-believed / **long**-distance / **long**-drawn / **long**-flowing / **long**-lost / **long**-pending / **long**-serving / **long**-shuttered / **long**-sought / **long**-standing / **long**-suppressed / **long**-time / **long**bow / **long**-delayed / **long**-established / **long**horn / **long**-lapsed /

long-last / **long**-lasting / **long**-life / **long**-lived / **long**-range / **long**-running / **long**-sighted / **long**-sightedness / **long**-suffering / **long**-term / **long**winded

Formation of Adjectives Using Combining Form '-LOOKING'

General meaning: to be appearing in the way that is mentioned

ADJECTIVES: expensive-**looking** / fearsome-**looking** / fine-**looking** / grave-**looking** / identical-**looking** / outward-**looking** / stern-**looking** / suspicious-**looking** / tired-**looking** / tough-**looking**

LIST OF 175 POPULAR 'COMBINING FORMS' THAT ARE USED TO MAKE ADJECTIVES:

afro- / agro- / all- / Anglo- / anthropo- / -appointed / -approved / -armed / astro- / audio- / Austro- / auto- / -backed / -bashing / -battered / -beaked / -bearing / -bedecked / bi- / biblio- / bio- / -born / -borne / -bound / -breaking / -built / -burning / cardio- / -caused / -cheeked / chrono- / -clad / -clothed / -consuming / contra- / -controlled / counter- / -covered / -cratic / -crippled / cross- / -cutting / cyber- / -deep and deep- / -deprived / -dimensional / -dominated / double- / -draped / -driven / dys- / eco- / -edged / electro- / -emitting / -enabled / -enhancing / -equipped / -eyed / fast- / -fed / -fflicted / -filled / -fired / -fitted / -flavored / -flowing / -footed / fore- / -free / -friendly / full- / -generating / geo- / -haired / half- / -headed / -hearted / -held / hepta- / hexa- / high- / -hit / homo- / hydro- / indo- / -induced / -infested / -inflicted / -issuing / italo- / -laced / -laden / -led / -like / -logical / -loving / low- / macro- / -made / -making / mal- / -marred / meta- / micro- / -minded / -monitored / mono- / -mouthed / much- / multi- / nano- / neo- / neuro- / -nosed / -obsessed / omni- / -operated / -oriented / ortho- / -owned / -packed / petro- / -phobic / photo- / physio- / -plagued / poly- / -powered / -prone / proto- / pseudo- / psychi- (or psycho-) / quadri- / quasi- / radio- / -raising / -ravaged / -related / retro- / -ridden / -riddled / russo- / -saving / -seeking / self- / -shaped / -sighted / Sino- / -sized / -skinned / -smeared / -soaked / socio- / -stained / -starved / -stricken / -struck / -style / super- / -tainted / techno- / tele- / -tempered / theo- / thermo- / -throwing / -tinted / -torn / -toting / tri- / uni- / -waving / well- / -wide / -wielding

04c. Using 'Word + To/And + Word'

(B1). Formation of Adjectives Using "WORD + TO + WORD"

Air-**to**-air

Air-**to**-ground

Air-**to**-surface

Back-**to**-front

Business-**to**-business

Day-**to**-day

Difficult-**to**-reach

Down **to** earth

Easy-**to**-understand

Face-**to**-face

Free-**to**-air

Ground-**to**-air

Hand-**to**-hand

Hand-**to**-mouth

Harder-**to**-get

Hard-**to**-reach

Hard-**to**-see

Hard-**to**-wash-off

Head-**to**-head

Heart-**to**-heart

House-**to**-house

Impossible-**to**-please

Impossible-**to**-resist

Person-**to**-person

Ready-**to**-eat

Ready-**to**-harvest

Ready-**to**-wear

Surface-**to**-air

Surface-**to**-surface

Up-**to**-the-minute

Wall-**to**-wall

Well-**to-**do

Example Sentences:
They have successfully flight-tested **air-to-air** *missile. (adjective: air-to-air | noun: missile)*
We are not involved in the **day-to-day** *operation* of his businesses. *(adjective: day-to-day | noun: operation)*

(B2). Formation of Adjectives Using "WORD + AND + WORD"

Bread-**and**-butter
Down **and** out
Half-**and**-half
Hit-**and**-miss
Hit-**and**-run
Hole-**and**-corner
Meet-**and**-greet
Nickel-**and**-dime
Out-**and**-out
Pen-**and**-ink
Pick-**and**-mix
Point-**and**-click
Point-**and**-shoot
Rough-**and**-ready
Smash-**and**-grab
Touch-**and**-go
Try-**and**-buy
Up-**and**-coming

Example Sentences:
A total of **50** winners were selected for the virtual **meet-and-greet** *sessions* with him. *(adjective: meet-and-greet | noun: sessions)*
Our **touch-and-go** *relationship* went on for years and years. *(adjective: touch-and-go | noun: relationship)*

(B3). Formation of Adjectives Using "WORD + TO + BE + WORD"

Yet-**to**-be constructed
Yet-**to**-be identified
Yet-**to**-be launched
Yet-**to**-be-enforced
Yet-**to**-be-named

Soon-**to**-be launch
Soon-**to**-be-independent
Soon-**to**-be-published
Soon-**to**-be-released

Not-**to**-be missed

Example Sentences:
He did not explain what his **yet-to-be-named** *political party's* plans are! *(adjective: yet-to-be-named | noun: political party)*
I really love the sleek design of this **soon-to-be-launch** *Smartphone.* *(adjective: soon-to-be-launch | noun: Smartphone)*
There are **not-to-be-missed** *shows* on new channel. *(adjective: not-to-be-missed | noun: shows)*

<u>04d.</u> <u>Using</u> 'Nouns/Verbs/<u>Other</u> <u>Adjectives</u>'

(C1). Adjectives formed from Nouns:

athlete -- athletic

chill -- chilly

cost -- costly

courtesy -- courteous

fool -- foolish

friend -- friendly

hair -- hairless

hedonist -- hedonistic

joy -- joyful

kitten -- kittenish

lady -- ladylike

law -- lawful

length -- lengthy

life -- lifeless

magic -- magical

month -- monthly

mystery -- mysterious

photograph -- photographic

poison -- poisonous

power -- powerful

science -- scientific

smell -- smelly

war -- warlike

width -- wide

Example Sentences (To Show Formation of Adjectives from Other Nouns):

Who is your favorite **athlete?** *(noun: athlete)*

Who is the vice president of the **athletic** *association? (adjective: athletic | noun: athlete)*

The **chill** which left us shivering is likely to decrease in next few days. *(noun: chill)*
Showers and **chilly** *temperatures* take us into the new work week. *(adjective: chilly | noun: temperatures)*

(C2). Adjectives formed from Verbs:
absorb -- absorbable
accept -- acceptable
damage -- damaging
enjoy -- enjoyable
escape -- escaping
generate -- generative
help --helpless
horrify -- horrifying
improve -- improved
laud -- laudable
manipulate -- manipulative
obey --obedient
play --playful
talk --talkative

Example Sentences (To Show Formation of Adjectives from Other Verbs):

Atoms of different elements **absorb** different wavelengths of light. *(verb: absorb)*
The **absorbable** *sutures* are highly useful in the treatment of inner organs surgical site closure. *(adjective: absorbable | noun: sutures)*

It is difficult to **accept** he is no more. *(verb: accept)*
Is this an **acceptable** *practice? (adjective: acceptable | noun: practice)*

(C3). Adjectives formed from other Adjectives:

comic -- comical

correct -- corrective

elder -- elderly

funny -- funniest

graceful -- disgraceful

high -- higher

incorrect -- incorrectly

red -- reddish

sick -- sickly

Example Sentences (To Show Formation of Adjectives from Other Adjectives):

Children like **comic** *books* and graphic novels. *(adjective: comic | noun: books)*

He gave me a few **comical** *suggestions* for my project. *(adjective: comical | noun: suggestions)*

Strict exercise regime without **correct** *diet* is unhelpful. *(adjective: correct | noun: diet)*

Reassess your actions and take **corrective** *steps. (adjective: corrective | noun: steps)*

04e. Using 'Adverbs'

You can also form adjectives using adverbs. Most of these adverbs are **-ly** words. You can add another word with **-ly** word to get the adjective. Note, all these adjectives are compound words.

Examples:
Spiritually charged
Specially designed
Socially conscious
Repeatedly used

Example Sentences *(Adjectives Used Attributively)*:
Her album is a collection of **spiritually charged** *songs. (adjective: spiritually charged | noun: songs)*
Policemen underwent a **specially designed** *course* with cognitive behavioral therapy. *(adjective: specially designed | noun: course)*
Many of us are becoming more **socially conscious** *consumers. (adjective: socially conscious | noun: consumers)*

Example Sentences *(Adjectives Used Predicatively)*:
*He was **academically bright.***

05. Important Notes

(1). THE SAME WORD IN DIFFERENT PARTS OF SPEECH

Some words can be two parts of speech. This is true for words that end in '-ed' and '-ing', such as 'elevated' and 'elevating'.

In the first and second sentences below, the words (**elevated** and **elevating**) are adjectives, while in the third and fourth sentence they are verbs. In the first sentence, '**elevated**' describes the word 'position', and in the second sentence '**elevating**' describes the word ´experience´.

1. His house is in **elevated** *position* (adjective)
2. Reading this book is an **elevating** *experience* (adjective)
3. Smoking **elevated** his blood pressure (verb)
4. He is **elevating** my spirits (verb)

(2). SOME ADJECTIVES HAVE TWO FORMS (ADJECTIVES ENDING IN '-IC' AND '-ICAL')

Some adjectives have only one form, e.g. basic, apolitical, astronomical but some adjectives have two forms with or without any difference in meaning:

Alphanumeric | Alphanumerical
Analytic | Analytical
Anarchic | Anarchical
Angelic | Angelical
Apathetic | Apathetical
Apocalyptic | Apocalyptical
Architectonic | Architectonical
Arithmetic | Arithmetical
Ascetic | Ascetical
Bibliographic | Bibliographical

Biometric | Biometrical
Biotic | Biotical
Bucolic | Bucolical
Classic | Classical
Demographic | Demographical
Diabolic | Diabolical
Didactic | Didactical
Dynamic | Dynamical
Economic | Economical
Electric | Electrical
Elliptic | Elliptical
Emblematic | Emblematical
Enigmatic | Enigmatical
Epidemic | Epidemical
Ethnographic | Ethnographical
Euphemistic | Euphemistical
Fantastic | Fantastical
Gastronomic | Gastronomical
Geographic | Geographical
Geometric | Geometrical
Graphic | Graphical
Hermetic | Hermetical
Historic | Historical
Hyperbolic | Hyperbolical
Idiomatic | Idiomatical
Mythic | Mythical
Parasitic | Parasitical
Periodic | Periodical
Photoelectric | Photoelectrical
Photographic | Photographical
Poetic | Poetical
Problematic | Problematical
Psychometric | Psychometrical
Symbolic | Symbolical
Symmetric | Symmetrical

Syntactic | Syntactical

Systematic | Systematical

(3). SOME ADJECTIVES CAN BE USED WITHOUT NOUNS!

Some adjectives can be used without nouns. Mind the definite article the:

the rich = rich people

the poor = poor people

Why do **the rich** have so much power?

When the price of rice is high, **the poor** cannot afford it.

(4). ADJECTIVES, ENDING IN '-ING' AND '-ED'

There are adjectives ending in -ing and -ed. These are participle constructions, used like adjectives.

Example Sentences:

(A). You can put adjective before the noun:

Go straight into the most **challenging** *problems.*

It is a **depressing** *situation* that we're in now.

He comes from a deeply **disturbed** *background.*

(B). You can put adjective after the verb:

It *was* **challenging** to work until the end.

This news *is* **depressing.**

I *got* **disturbed** seeing his agony.

<u>About the Author</u>

Manik Joshi was born on January 26, 1979 at Ranikhet, a picturesque town in the Kumaon region of the Indian state of Uttarakhand. He is permanent resident of the Sheeshmahal area of Kathgodam located in the city of Haldwani in the Kumaon region of Uttarakhand in India. He completed his schooling in four different schools. He is a science graduate in the ZBC – zoology, botany, and chemistry – subjects. He is also an MBA with a specialization in marketing. Additionally, he holds diplomas in "computer applications", "multimedia and web-designing", and "computer hardware and networking". During his schooldays, he wanted to enter the field of medical science; however, after graduation he shifted his focus to the field of management. After obtaining his MBA, he enrolled in a computer education center; he became so fascinated with working on the computer that he decided to develop his career in this field. Over the following years, he worked at some computer-related full-time jobs. Following that, he became interested in Internet Marketing, particularly in domaining (business of buying and selling domain names), web design (creating websites), and various other online jobs. However, later he shifted his focus solely to self-publishing. Manik is a nature-lover. He has always been fascinated by overcast skies. He is passionate about traveling and enjoys solo-travel most of the time rather than traveling in groups. He is actually quite a loner who prefers to do his own thing. He likes to listen to music, particularly when he is working on the computer. Reading and writing are definitely his favorite pastimes, but he has no interest in sports. Manik has always dreamed of a prosperous life and prefers to live a life of luxury. He has a keen interest in politics because he believes it is politics that decides everything else. He feels a sense of gratification sharing his experiences and knowledge with the outside world. However, he is an introvert by nature and thus gives prominence to only a few people in his personal life. He is not a spiritual man, yet he actively seeks knowledge about the metaphysical world; he is particularly interested in learning about life beyond death. In addition to writing academic/informational text and fictional content, he also maintains a personal diary. He has always had a desire to stand out from the crowd. He does not believe in treading the beaten path and avoids copying someone else's path to success. Two things he always refrains from are smoking and drinking; he is a teetotaler and very health-conscious. He usually wakes up before the sun rises. He starts his morning with meditation and exercise. Fitness is an integral and indispensable part of his life. He gets energized by solving complex problems. He loves himself the way he is and he loves the way he looks. He doesn't believe in following fashion trends. He dresses according to what suits him & what he is comfortable in. He believes in taking calculated risks. His philosophy is to expect the best but prepare for the worst. According to him, you can't succeed if you are unwilling to fail. For Manik, life is about learning from mistakes and figuring out how to move forward.

Amazon Author Page of Manik Joshi:
https://www.amazon.com/author/manikjoshi
Website: http://www.manikjoshi.com
Email: manik85joshi@gmail.com

BIBLIOGRAPHY

(A). SERIES TITLE: "ENGLISH DAILY USE" *[40 BOOKS]*

01. How to Start a Sentence
02. English Interrogative Sentences
03. English Imperative Sentences
04. Negative Forms in English
05. Learn English Exclamations
06. English Causative Sentences
07. English Conditional Sentences
08. Creating Long Sentences in English
09. How to Use Numbers in Conversation
10. Making Comparisons in English
11. Examples of English Correlatives
12. Interchange of Active and Passive Voice
13. Repetition of Words
14. Remarks in English Language
15. Using Tenses in English
16. English Grammar- Am, Is, Are, Was, Were
17. English Grammar- Do, Does, Did
18. English Grammar- Have, Has, Had
19. English Grammar- Be and Have
20. English Modal Auxiliary Verbs
21. Direct and Indirect Speech
22. Get- Popular English Verb
23. Ending Sentences with Prepositions
24. Popular Sentences in English
25. Common English Sentences
26. Daily Use English Sentences
27. Speak English Sentences Everyday
28. Popular English Idioms and Phrases
29. Common English Phrases
30. Daily English- Important Notes
31. Collocations in English Language
32. Words That Act as Multiple Parts of Speech (Part 1)
33. Words That Act as Multiple Parts of Speech (Part 2)
34. Nouns In English Language
35. Regular and Irregular Verbs
36. Transitive and Intransitive Verbs

37. 10,000 Useful Adjectives in English
38. 4,000 Useful Adverbs in English
39. 20 Categories of Transitional Expressions
40. How to End a Sentence

****

(B). SERIES TITLE: "ENGLISH WORD POWER" *[30 BOOKS]*

01. Dictionary of English Synonyms
02. Dictionary of English Antonyms
03. Homonyms, Homophones and Homographs
04. Dictionary of English Capitonyms
05. Dictionary of Prefixes and Suffixes
06. Dictionary of Combining Forms
07. Dictionary of Literary Words
08. Dictionary of Old-fashioned Words
09. Dictionary of Humorous Words
10. Compound Words in English
11. Dictionary of Informal Words
12. Dictionary of Category Words
13. Dictionary of One-word Substitution
14. Hypernyms and Hyponyms
15. Holonyms and Meronyms
16. Oronym Words in English
17. Dictionary of Root Words
18. Dictionary of English Idioms
19. Dictionary of Phrasal Verbs
20. Dictionary of Difficult Words
21. Dictionary of Verbs
22. Dictionary of Adjectives
23. Dictionary of Adverbs
24. Dictionary of Formal Words
25. Dictionary of Technical Words
26. Dictionary of Foreign Words
27. Dictionary of Approving & Disapproving Words
28. Dictionary of Slang Words
29. Advanced English Phrases
30. Words In English Language

****

<u>(C). SERIES TITLE: "WORDS IN COMMON USAGE"</u> *[10 BOOKS]*

01. How to Use the Word "Break" in English
02. How to Use the Word "Come" in English
03. How to Use the Word "Go" in English
04. How to Use the Word "Have" in English
05. How to Use the Word "Make" in English
06. How to Use the Word "Put" in English
07. How to Use the Word "Run" in English
08. How to Use the Word "Set" in English
09. How to Use the Word "Take" in English
10. How to Use the Word "Turn" in English

****

<u>(D). SERIES TITLE: "WORDS BY NUMBER OF LETTERS"</u> *[10 BOOKS]*

01. Dictionary of 4-Letter Words
02. Dictionary of 5-Letter Words
03. Dictionary of 6-Letter Words
04. Dictionary of 7-Letter Words
05. Dictionary of 8-Letter Words
06. Dictionary of 9-Letter Words
07. Dictionary of 10-Letter Words
08. Dictionary of 11-Letter Words
09. Dictionary of 12- to 14-Letter Words
10. Dictionary of 15- to 18-Letter Words

****

<u>(E). SERIES TITLE: "ENGLISH WORKSHEETS"</u> *[10 BOOKS]*

01. English Word Exercises (Part 1)
02. English Word Exercises (Part 2)
03. English Word Exercises (Part 3)
04. English Sentence Exercises (Part 1)
05. English Sentence Exercises (Part 2)
06. English Sentence Exercises (Part 3)
07. Test Your English
08. Match the Two Parts of the Words
09. Letter-Order In Words
10. Choose the Correct Spelling

www.ingramcontent.com/pod-product-compliance
Lightning Source LLC
Chambersburg PA
CBHW031129250726
48655CB00002B/580